Christianity, as the auth[...] threatened not only by th[...] gions of capitalism and nationalism, but is even now in America becoming a purely national religion, unintelligible to Christians of other lands, as their Protestantism is becoming unintelligible to us. This may be, they say, the beginning of a process which already in Germany has resulted in a new national religion.

The only hope they see for the salvation of the church is a strong reaffirmation of its primary purpose, to witness to and be a revealer of the true and universal Christian faith: that God is not made in man's image, but transcends man just as his purposes for man transcend humanism, nationalism, social welfare, and all the current creeds of the day. The " social gospel " as the primary concern of the church comes in for a drastic criticism. The task of the church is nothing less than to proclaim a gospel which is timeless and universal — true for all men in all ages and places. If the church contents itself with any lesser task it is doomed as the instrument of God — even though it survive as a human institution.

THE CHURCH AGAINST THE WORLD

THE CHURCH
AGAINST
THE WORLD

H. RICHARD NIEBUHR
Associate Professor of Christian Ethics, Yale University

WILHELM PAUCK
Professor of Church History,
The Chicago Theological Seminary

FRANCIS P. MILLER
Chairman, The World Student Christian Federation

WILLETT, CLARK & COMPANY
CHICAGO   NEW YORK
1935

CONTENTS

INTRODUCTION

By H. Richard Niebuhr

THE QUESTION OF THE CHURCH

THE title of our book is not so much the enunciation of a theme as it is the declaration of a position. We are seeking not to expound a thesis but to represent a point of view and to raise a question. The point of view is from within the church, is that of churchmen who, having been born into the Christian community, having been nurtured in it and having been convinced of the truth of its gospel, know no life apart from it. It is, moreover, the point of view of those who find themselves within a *threatened* church. The world has always been against the church, but there have been times when the world has been partially converted, and when the church has lived with it in some measure of peace; there have been other times when the world was more or less openly hostile, seeking to convert the church. We live, it is evident, in a time of hostility when the church is imperiled not only by an external worldliness but by one that has established itself within the Christian camp. Our position is inside a church which has been on the retreat and which has made compromises with the enemy in thought, in organization, and in discipline.

I

Finally, our position is in the midst of that increasing group in the church which has heard the command to halt, to remind itself of its mission, and to await further orders.

The question which we raise in this situation may best be stated in the gospel phrase, " What must we do to be saved? " The " we " in this question does not refer to our individual selves, as though we were isolated persons who could have a life apart from the church or apart from the nation and the race. It denotes rather the collective self, the Christian community. In an earlier, individualistic time evangelical Christians raised the question of their salvation one by one, and we cannot quarrel with them; they realized the nature of their problem as it appeared to them in their own day. Today, however, we are more aware of the threat against our collective selves than of that against our separate souls. We are asking: " What must we the nation, or we the class, or we the race do to be saved? " It is in this sense that we ask, " What must we the church do to be saved? " It is true that the authors of these brief essays have no commission to ask the question for others, nor to raise it as though they conceived themselves as spokesmen of the church. Yet they can and must ask it, as responsible members

2

of the body of Christ, who believe that many of their fellow members are asking it also, and that the time has come for an active awareness of and discussion of its meaning.

The point of view represented and the question raised are to be distinguished, we believe, from those of many of our contemporaries who look at the church from the outside. Though some of these are members, yet they do not seem to be committed to the church, and they appear to direct their questions to it rather than to raise them as members of the community. They seem to criticize the church by reference to some standard which is not the church's but that of civilization or of the world. Apparently they require the church to engage in a program of salvation which is not of a piece with the church's gospel. They demand that it become a savior, while the church has always known that it is not a savior but the company of those who have found a savior. These critics have a right to be heard. A church which knows that it is not self-sufficient nor secure in righteousness but dependent on God for judgment and renewal as well as for life will expect him to use as instruments of his judgment the opponents and critics of Christianity. Yet the judgment of the outsider is not the final judgment

3

of God, and his standard is not the divine standard for the church. An individual can profit greatly by the criticism of his fellows yet he will realize that they are judging him by standards which are neither his own nor God's, that he is both a worse and a better man than their judgments indicate, and that the greatest service they can render him is to call him back to his own best self. He will realize that he is not under any obligation to conform to the ideals which his friends or his critics set up for him, but that he is indeed obligated to be true to his own ideal. It is so with the church. Much as it may profit by the criticisms of those outside, it must not forget that they are asking it to conform to principles not its own, and endeavoring to use it for ends foreign to its nature. The question of the church, seen from the inside, is not how it can measure up to the expectations of society nor what it must do to become a savior of civilization, but rather how it can be true to itself: that is, to its Head. What must it do to be saved?

This question is not a selfish one; it is only the question of a responsible self. Critics of the gospel of salvation, who characterize it as self-centered and intent upon self-satisfaction, thoroughly misunderstand the sources and the bearing of the cry for

4

salvation. In the period of individualism, persons sought redemption not because they desired pleasures in " the by-and-by " but because they found themselves on the road to futility, demoralization, and destructiveness. Because they were concerned with their own impotence in good works and with the harm they were doing to others, they were not less altruistic than those who were concerned only with doing good, and inattentive to the evil consequences of many good works. The avowed altruists were not less selfish than seekers after salvation just because they wished to be saviors rather than saved. Nor is it true that the desire for salvation is unsocial. It arises — for the church today as for individuals in all times — not in solitariness but within the social nexus. The church has seen all mankind involved in crisis and has sought to offer help — only to discover the utter insufficiency of its resources. Confronting the poverty, the warfare, the demoralization of human life, it has sought within itself for the wisdom and the power with which to give aid, and has discovered its impotence. Therefore it must cry, " What must I do to be saved? " It has made pronouncements against war, promoted schemes for peace, leagues of nations, pacts for the outlawry of war, associations for international friendship, organizations of war resisters; but the march of Mars is halted not for a moment by the petty impediments placed in its way. The church has set up programs of social justice, preached utopian ideals, adopted resolutions, urged charity, proclaimed good will among men; but neither the progressive impoverishment of the life of the many nor the growth of the privileges of the few has been stayed by its efforts. It has set up schemes of moral and religious education, seeking to inculcate brotherly love, to draw forth sympathetic good will, to teach self-discipline; but the progress of individual and social disintegration goes on. The church knows that the meaning of its life lies in the service it can give to God's creatures. It cannot abandon its efforts to help. Yet, looking upon the inadequacy and the frequent futility of its works, how can it help but cry, "What must I do to be saved?"

The question has another and more positive source. The church has been made to realize not only the ineffectiveness but the harmfulness of much of its labor. The individual raises the question of his salvation, rather than that of his savior-hood, when he faces the fact that he is not only not a Messiah but actually a sinner; that he is profiting

6

by, consenting to, and sharing in man's inhumanity to man; that he is not the man upon the cross but one of the crowd beneath. So, the church has discovered that it belongs to the crucifiers rather than to the crucified; that all talk of becoming a martyr in the cause of good will, some time in the future, is but wishful thinking with little relevance to present reality. Its outside critics have taxed the church with giving opium to the people, and with securing its own position as well as that of its allies by preaching contentment to the poor. Had it been poor as Jesus was poor, had it identified itself with those to whom it preached contentment, had it not profited by the system of distribution which brings poverty, its conscience would have been clear. It would have been able to respond that it had preached nothing which it had not practiced. But being what it is, the church has been unable to refute the charge with a wholly good conscience. It knows that it has often been an obstruction in the path of social change and that it has tried to maintain systems of life which men and God had condemned to death. Its outside critics have held the church responsible for the increase of nationalism. They have pointed to the role of Protestantism, Pietism, and even of Catholicism in fostering the sense of national des-

7

tiny, in giving religious sanction to the imperialist programs of kings and democracies, in justifying nationalist wars and in blessing armies bound on conquest. The church stands convicted of this sin without being at all confident that it has found out how to resist similar temptations in the future. At all events, it knows that it has been on the side of the slayers rather than of the slain. The critics have reminded the church of its part in the development of that economic system which, whatever its virtues, has revealed its vices so clearly to our times that none can take pride in having assisted it to success, in however innocent a role. The harm which the church has done and is doing in these and other areas of human life may be greatly exaggerated in its adversaries' indictments. But no section of the church can plead " not guilty " to all the counts. Convicted by its conscience more than by its foes, it joins the penitents at its own altars, asking, " What must we do to be saved? "

In the crisis of the world the church becomes aware of its own crisis: not that merely of a weak and responsible institution but of one which is threatened with destruction. It is true, as Francis Miller points out in his essay, that the church will probably survive in some form in any circumstances,

8

and that the real question is whether it will survive as a reliable witness to the Christian faith. Yet it is also true that the larger question receives part of its urgency from the threat of extinction. It was when Israel's life as a nation was in danger that the prophets came to understand the more dire peril to Israel as a people of God. The knowledge of death played a part in the conversions of Augustine and Luther. So the church is being awakened to its inner crisis by the external one in which it is involved. It has seen enough of the indifference or hostility of the world, and of the defeats of some of its component parts, to realize that its continuance in the world is by no means a certainty. It knows the ways of God too well not to understand that he can and will raise up another people to carry out the mission entrusted to it if the Christian community fail him. It cannot look to the future with assurance that it carries a guarantee of immortality. The knowledge of the external crisis — in which as an institution it must become increasingly involved — may lead it to inquire first into the conditions of physical survival. Yet a society based, as the church has been, upon the conviction that to seek life is to lose it, must discover the fallacy in any attempt merely to live for the sake of living. Like any Christian individual

9

faced with death, the church then realizes that the important question is not how to save its life but rather how to keep its soul, how to face loss, impoverishment, and even death without surrendering its self, its work, and its service.

From the point of view of civilization the question of the church seems often to be regarded as that of an institution which has failed to adjust itself to the world and which is making desperate efforts to overcome its maladjustments. The problem it presents is that of a conservative organization which has not kept abreast of the times, which has remained medieval while the world was growing modern, dogmatic while civilization was becoming scientific; which is individualistic in a collectivist period and theological in a time of humanism. The answer, it is thought, must come from science, politics, history, civilization. If the church is intent on being saved, then, from this point of view, it must direct its question to civilization. But within the church the problem has a different aspect. There is a sense, to be sure, in which the church must adjust itself to the world in which it lives and become all things to all men in order that it may win some. It is true also, within certain limits, that failure to adjust results in decay as is evident in all mere traditionalism.

But the desire to become all things to all men still presupposes a faith which does not change and a gospel to which they are to be won. The failure of traditionalism, moreover, is less in its lack of adjustment to changing conditions than in the confusion of the spirit with the letter and in blindness to the actual shift of attention from meaning to symbol that has taken place within the church.

In the faith of the church, the problem is not one of adjustment to the changing, relative, and temporal elements in civilization but rather one of constant adjustment, amid these changing things, to the eternal. The crisis of the church from this point of view is not the crisis of the church in the world, but of the world in the church. What is endangered in the church is the secular element: its prestige as a social institution, its power as a political agency, its endowment as a foster-child of nation or of class. And this very peril indicates that the church has adjusted itself too much rather than too little to the world in which it lives. It has identified itself too intimately with capitalism, with the philosophy of individualism, and with the imperialism of the West. Looking to the future, the danger of the church lies more in a readiness to adjust itself to new classes, races, or national civilizations than in refusal to accept them. This moment of crisis, between a worldliness that is passing and a worldliness that is coming, is the moment of the church's opportunity to turn away from its temporal toward its eternal relations and so to become fit again for its work in time.

From the point of view of the church, moreover, the threat against it is being made not by a changing world but by an unchanging God. The " cracks in time " which now appear are fissures too deep for human contriving, and reveal a justice too profound to be the product of chance. The God who appears in this judgment of the world is neither the amiable parent of the soft faith we recently avowed nor the miracle worker of a superstitious supernaturalism; he is rather the eternal God, Creator, Judge, and Redeemer, whom prophets and apostles heard, and saw at work, casting down and raising up. He uses all things temporal as his instruments, but resigns his sovereignty to none. Hence the fear of the church is not inspired by men but by the living God, and it directs its question not to the changing world with its self-appointed messiahs but to its sovereign Lord.

Because this is true the church can raise the question of the church but cannot answer it. It knows where to go to hear the answer; it cannot specify at what time or in what way that answer will come: so that it will be compelled to obedience by the authority of the word and the conviction in its heart. It knows that it must go to the place of penitence. It knows that it must go into silence and quiet. It knows that it must go to the Scriptures, not in worship of the letter, but because this is the place where it is most likely to hear the reverberations of that commandment and that promise which sent it on its way.

The following essays are variations upon this theme or, since none of us is empowered to speak for the others, this introduction may be considered as a variation upon a theme stated more clearly in one of the subsequent parts. We have not sought to define closely our common point of view. We wish only to add our contributions to a task which seems to us all-important, the task of the Christian community in defining and taking its position against the world.

PART ONE
By Wilhelm Pauck

THE CRISIS OF RELIGION

IT is likely that at all times in human history many men and women have spent their lives unaware of the deeper meanings of existence. But surely there have been few historical periods in which men were so disillusioned about the meaningfulness of life as they are in our own era. A majority of our contemporaries seem to lead the existence of drifters. They perform perfunctorily those " duties " which lie immediately at hand; they struggle grimly for " a place in the sun " for themselves and their own. They seem unconscious of any peculiarly human dignity — if such consciousness involves active and resolute participation in a meaningful process of the whole universe. Depth seems to be the one dimension strangely absent from the life of the present generation. A spirit of uncertainty has shaken, it seems, all positive convictions. The most urgent human concern appears to be " security." All political movements, economic and cultural discussions, and religious longings are directed toward the overcoming of the feeling of " insecurity " which is abroad in all lands. The world-wide depression is not primarily economic but psychological in character. The morale of present-day mankind is not that of builders of civilization. There are comparatively few who can say *how* a civilization should be built and there are many who ask *why* it should be built anyway.

When we ask ourselves how this situation has come about we answer, usually, that we are experiencing a crisis of civilization, that we are living in the end of an era, that we are members of a period of cultural transition. History indicates that cultural crises arise when men grow uncertain of the validity of the principles which determine their cultural activities, when they cannot look with confidence into the future. As far as I can see, there are three typical interpretations of this situation. The first is that of the pessimists. Oswald Spengler, author of the famous work, *The Decline of the West*, may be considered an absolute pessimist. On the basis of a philosophy of history which interprets cultures as quasi-organic units undergoing development from youth through maturity to decline, and on the basis of a comparison of the stages in the growth of world-civilizations, he concludes that Western civilization has exhausted its productive powers. The technical, metropolitan, militarist, organizational nature of our present civilization is proof of its decay. The astonishing similarities between our age and that of the declining Roman Empire make it necessary that we reconcile ourselves to the inevitable destiny of complete cultural disintegration. Western civilization will be superseded by a new culture which will arise in other parts of the earth. Whether this future leadership lies in Russia or among the colored races, no one can tell. Although significant criticisms can be raised against this interpretation, especially because Spengler has overlooked the fact of historical continuity, it cannot be denied that the mood of heroic despair which he expresses is widespread in the Western world.

H. G. Wells's *The Shape of Things To Come* is an example of relative pessimism. In so far as he sees forces at work which seem to prepare the way for a world-state — namely, economic and cultural interdependence among all people of the earth — his outlook is hopeful. But because of the present strength of those powers which counteract the tendencies toward a unification of the world — primarily nationalism and politics dominated by the principle of the sovereignty of the state — he is pessimistic about the next decades. For he believes that these anti-democratic, anti-universalistic, fascist powers will call forth a long chain of world-conflicts. He is persuaded that they will not yield to the world-unifying powers without a struggle for life and death. But they will inevitably destroy themselves, and the world-state of the future will arise only on their ruins. The generations of the present day and of the near future will therefore need to suffer vicariously for the benefit of their great-grandchildren and their more fortunate descendants. This speculative fatalism does not appear absolutely impossible to one who considers the present state of the world realistically. Prophets of doom, however, have been wrong more frequently than right. One cannot depend upon their opinions. Furthermore, human nature is so constructed that it will not accept a positive or negative fatalism. In his freedom to make vital decisions, man will act to change those tendencies in his civilization which he recognizes as leading him to his doom.

The second group of interpreters of the present crisis are fully aware of this characteristically human possibility. They are the revolutionaries. Overcome by the knowledge that the social order does not permit the full realization of social justice or that the rulers of the present system will not yield

to the just demand of economically, socially or politically vanquished masses and groups, they work
for the destruction of a cultural order which has
proved to be sick and unproductive. By smashing
an old order they hope to pave the way for a new
one. It is not impossible that the cultural crisis of
our day will issue in a world-revolution. Many
among us speak of "the coming struggle for
power" between fascism and communism. But it
must be evident that even a "successful revolution"
destroys more than it builds, and that, when the
revolutionists are compelled to engage in construction, they are forced to obey the laws of historical
continuity by adjusting themselves to the world as
it is and has been. The history of the Bolshevist
revolution in Russia exemplifies this fact.

Finally, there is a third group of leaders who are
neither pessimists nor revolutionaries. They speak
and act with a sense of true historical responsibility.
Recognizing that men are part of an historical process from which they cannot escape, they also know
that human culture is the result of human decisions
made in constructive reaction to the process and
with a view to man's physical and spiritual welfare.
They remember that our own Western civilization
has run so far through two main phases of develop-

ment: the so-called "medieval" feudalist form of life (the last remnants of which are still effective in certain parts of our civilization, in the monarchic governments, for example) was superseded by the bourgeois culture, which has determined the so-called "modern" period of history and of which we are the heirs. Because the creative possibilities of the fundamental principles of this second phase of Western civilization have been exhausted we are experiencing the present crisis. These principles are commonly called "self-determination" and "profit system." They came to life in the medieval towns, flourished first in the period of the Renaissance, and finally reached their highest expression in our modern scientific, technical, economic, imperialistic civilization.

It cannot be doubted that the modern world is what it is because it has cultivated and practiced the doctrine of the self-determination of man. It is the self-determined mind which has called "modern" philosophy into being, has produced "modern" science, has given the drive to "modern" economics and constantly nourished the spirit of capitalism, has caused the "modern" inventions to be made, and has created and sustained the political democracies. All these undeniably great achievements of the " modern " spirit have been extended to the ends of the world because the autonomous character of this spirit was effectively coupled with a restless acquisitiveness. But it has now become clear to an ever increasing number of our contemporaries all over the world that this " profit system " of a " rugged individualism " must be replaced by an order which, without sacrificing the values and attainments of bourgeois culture, is impelled by a new cultural temper.

If it were possible to define this new temper, the most significant step toward the overcoming of the crisis would have been taken. It may require the thought and action of more than one generation to develop this new sense of cultural responsibility. We can be true contemporaries of our era only if we recognize the historical place in which we find ourselves. This means that we must be willing to admit that what is happening today in America, Italy, Germany, Russia, and all countries, is a series of expressions of the crisis itself.

Of the programs which are now being developed in the different parts of the world none, I think, can be considered a definitely hopeful, truly constructive, absolutely " satisfactory " measure. New cultural building will begin only when more men and women recognize the religious nature of the cultural crisis. The self-determined civilization of the last centuries is disintegrating because it does not correspond to the divine (i.e., universally meaningful) order of things. I do not wish to use merely a pious phrase when I say that we are now in our difficult situation because the hand of God is upon us. We must be ready again to listen to the voice which calls to us: " Repent ye, for the Kingdom of God is at hand."

It is just at this point, however, that the most disturbing aspect of the crisis becomes apparent. We are uncertain of our readiness to listen to this call, for we have lost confidence even in those institutions and practices which nourish and express the religious spirit. It can hardly be doubted that the Christian church as well as civilization is at present in a state of crisis, for it also is beset by uncertainty as to its own sufficiency. Consequently, the church is not sure of its message or of the methods by which that message can be brought to people at home and abroad. It recognizes, with resultant loss of confidence in itself, that it is being subjected to critical examination.

It may be enlightening to observe that in its history Christianity has undergone several crises of

24

a similar nature.[1]   They all were successfully over-come, but each of the crises of the past has led in some direct way to the critical state of affairs in the church of the present day.

The symptoms of a crisis in Christianity, con-sisting of the loss of the certainty of its absolute validity, appeared first of all during the Middle Ages in consequence of the Crusades.   Whatever the causes of these great adventures, they were un-dertaken with the sanction and under the leadership of the Roman Catholic church.   They were looked upon as an expression of the power of papal univer-salism; the popes and churchmen who sponsored these enterprises hoped that they would dem-onstrate to the whole world the strength of the church's control over the lives of the believers.   But the actual effect was an opposite one.   Instead of increasing the confidence of Christendom in its church, the Crusades caused the rise of movements and ideas which shook the sacramental, hierarchical institution to its foundations.   Heretical move-ments (e.g., the Albigenses) were organized under

[1] The following historical analysis was suggested by the lec-ture of H. Frick on *Die Krise der Religion* (Giessen, Topel-mann, 1931).   The whole article may be considered as an effort to describe the religious situation as it appears to an American observer.   It was inspired by a reading of Frick's lecture, written from the German point of view.

the direct influence of the new contact of the Western peoples with the East. A new social economic spirit, expressing itself in the rise of commercial towns and of a new social class, emerged in the Christian world. To be sure, the church succeeded in making the necessary adjustments, but it was difficult to ban a spirit of enlightenment which spread under the influence of foreign cultures upon the Christian civilization and which furthered the growth of skeptical attitudes toward the absolute validity of the ecclesiastical institution of redemption. The situation was saved by the piety which is best represented by St. Francis. The church made the wisest possible move by incorporating the new monasticism into itself. The world-ruling church of Innocent III received a new religious sanction from the most human and most Christlike of all the saints. The famous painting by Giotto which shows St. Francis upholding a basilica, no longer resting safely upon its own foundation, clearly suggests this idea. The Roman organization was supported by the devotion of those who lived for the ideal of the *imitatio Christi*. Henceforth, the unified Christian civilization could continue under the protectorate of the Roman bishop. Apparently the crisis had been overcome.

Its effects, however, continued to accompany the life of the church during the next centuries, until in the Renaissance and Reformation the sickness broke out again. The Renaissance was the expression of the spirit of the lay world which, in the towns and cities, had first emerged as a new and partly foreign element in the structure of medieval Christian society. The Reformation rapidly developed into a movement of violent criticism directed against the absolute authority of the ecclesiastical organization. The Roman church with its hierarchy and its sacraments, outside of which there was supposed to be no salvation in the name of Jesus Christ, was under fire. The fact that separate Protestant churches were soon formed necessarily raised the question: How could Christianity continue to offer the only salvation to mankind, particularly in view of the belief that this salvation was obtainable only in the society of those who called themselves the church? Luther and the reformers solved the problem by their teaching concerning the church. They distinguished between its visible and invisible forms. Only those who represented the invisible communion of saints, living by faith in the word of the gospel and in love of their fellow men, inspired by fellowship with God, formed the true Christian church. This distinction between essential or perfect, and unessential or imperfect, features in the church mitigated somewhat the bad effect of the division of Christianity and of its radical separation into two bodies which, by practicing an irreconcilable hostility, might endanger the cultivation of the Christian religion as such.

But the evolution of distinct Protestant bodies, which enhanced their claim to individuality by the formulation of new creeds and the construction of creedal theologies, soon led to a division within Protestantism itself. The sixteenth and seventeenth centuries especially witnessed a perennial strife of the evangelical groups with each other, which almost completely overshadowed their common contrast to the Roman church from which they had both seceded. This intra-Protestant conflict did not cease even during the Wars of Religion, in which the ecclesiastical conflict of the Reformation period was carried into the political arena. With the rise of a new cultural movement during the eighteenth century, commonly known as the Enlightenment, a new critic of the church but one which was also a helper appeared on the scene.

Out of a spirit similar to that of modern America, which is inclined to repudiate denominational religion, the men of the Age of Reason tended to consider the churches incapable of furnishing them with that religious life which was needed, since they worked for the destruction of each other in the name of their creeds, while all of them claimed to serve the one Lord, Jesus Christ. Furthermore, the development of the modern sciences, and particularly of philosophy and history, brought about an entirely new view of religion and Christianity. The apparent moral weakness and inefficiency of the creedal churches, together with the wider knowledge of the religions of foreign and ancient peoples, produced in many minds a critical attitude toward the church, comparable in many ways to the situation which had threatened the medieval establishment centuries before. The problem of the finality of Christianity now became really pressing. Under the impact of the historical comparison of religions, undertaken with ever increasing effectiveness, and in consequence of a rational analysis of the dogmas and creeds, the church was about to lose its power over the hearts of men. The protests of the orthodox groups were in vain; in vain also was the revival of religious emotionalism in the various groups of Pietism upon the Continent. The Christian church was face to face with a crisis more radical and dangerous than any that had arisen in the past. Indeed, it has been latent within Christendom ever since.

But again the situation was saved. The cure was effected by methods very similar in character to those which had proved helpful in the crises of the past. It must be observed that in the crises so far discussed the physicians appeared within the church itself. Each time the crisis was felt first of all in the ranks of outsiders who, seeing the weaknesses of the church, proceeded to treat it with indifference and contempt while they cultivated those forces which had shaken the confidence of the church in itself. Thus the church was never led into the road to recovery by the efforts of these critics, but rather by the contribution of those who, filled with the fresh spirit of new times, reformed the Christian religion from within. It was not Frederick II who came to the rescue of the medieval church, but St. Francis, the product of town-society. Not the leaders of the Renaissance and not the Humanists of the sixteenth century saved the church from destruction, but Martin Luther, the revolutionary and the arch-heretic. Similarly, it was not Voltaire, the most prominent among the literary critics of Christianity in the eighteenth century, who suggested constructive means by which healing might be effected, but men of the type of Schleiermacher, Maurice, Kingsley, Robertson, Bushnell, Chalmers, Wichern, Rauschenbusch. Thoroughly in harmony with the mood of their time, they set about to suggest to the Christians ideas by which they could understand themselves in a new way. Just as the medieval church did not need to undo the effects of the Crusades in order to benefit by the spirit of holiness exhibited by St. Francis and his kind, and just as Luther maintained the belief in the truth of Christianity without sacrificing any part of the new life which had become apparent in his reformation, so Schleiermacher and the modern interpreters of Christianity did not cease to be loyal to the new age when they taught the church a new understanding of itself, sufficient for the maintenance of faith in its own validity.

These saving new ideas have been characteristic of modern Protestantism to the present day. In various ways and with increasing directness, they have been asserted by modern Protestant thinkers. Their content, to describe them very simply, may be said to affirm the validity of Christianity in so far as it assures the fulfilment of life or the best possible moral living. In other words, the Christian religion is now no longer described as the true faith because it represents a supernatural revelation of God on which the absolute authority of the church or the Bible or the person of Jesus can be based. It is now defended on the basis of personal religious experience and on the ground of an analysis of its essence in which the supremacy of its moral character is disclosed. Thus modern theology has devoted a major part of its work to the proof of the thesis that in Christianity mankind is given the best guarantee of the highest and purest life. It can hardly be doubted that the defense of this thesis led not only to the overcoming of the eighteenth century crisis but also to the silencing of many questions concerning the validity of the Christian religion, which, during the nineteenth and twentieth centuries, were continually revived under the assault of the transformed world-view fostered by the development of science, technics and industry. Up to this day, Protestant apologetics depends largely upon the claim that only with the help of " religion " can the highest morality be sustained.

Now another religious crisis has arisen. Its appearance is due to the fact that this solution of the problem of the absoluteness of Christianity no longer suffices. For, in the meantime, there has emerged a secularism which claims to represent the same high moral ideals that Christianity does, but without dependence upon the religious beliefs which are characteristic of the church. Christianity is now face to face with an enemy more dangerous than any of the past. It is an atheistic movement which claims to cultivate moral ideals of the same value as those defended by the church. The modern crisis of religion is therefore caused by the conviction of many of our contemporaries that man can lead the good life without believing in God.

A closer analysis of this situation is necessary for the understanding of all its aspects. First of all, it must be pointed out that the rise of atheism is an almost unprecedented phenomenon. It is difficult to say at what time it became respectable, so to speak. But it is clear that even the most ardent enemies of the church who appeared during the eighteenth century, and won their outstanding triumphs in the French Revolution, rarely went so far as to identify their hostility against church and religion with the denial of God. The change occurred during the last century, when, particularly in France, public opinion became outspokenly atheistic and when, especially in Germany, Marxian socialism grew more and more into a definitely antireligious and

33

irreligious movement. The climax of this development was reached in the establishment of the Soviet regime in Russia, which has now become the most powerful political exponent of atheism in the world.

All this, of course, is only the most radical expression of a change of mind which has been characteristic of the development of Western civilization since the days of the Renaissance and Enlightenment. For the history of the modern Western mind may be said to be the history of a gradual secularization of man. Its outcome is apparent in the total structure of contemporary life, which as a whole moves along without a profound challenge from the spirit of religion, especially in so far as belief in God is implied. If that typical product of the modern age, the newspaper, can be considered an adequate mirror of the life of modern society, the world of religion has now been relegated to an insignificant corner in the existence of man, which is otherwise determined by the events and decisions in the fields of politics, business, sport and art.

This transformation has naturally not taken place without profound effect upon theology. During the sixteenth and seventeenth centuries a theological writer could assume that belief in God was a common and firm conviction; he could devote his arguments chiefly to the problems which necessarily follow from such a conviction. But since the beginning of the last century the fundamental theme of theological works is the question: Is there a God? — a question which, in the days of the past, was treated by way of prolegomena to the truly significant, constructive, theological discussions. It appears also that up to a recent past the preacher addressing his congregation could presuppose that its members were rooted in the belief in God. Modern sermons, however, seem to be directed chiefly to the end of communicating the conviction that the truly good life can be attained only by means of belief in God. A majority of modern sermons are arguments for a belief in God rather than exhortations, meditations or expositions which presuppose such a belief from the very outset. From this point of view, the baffling predilection for the word " religion " which seems to characterize most contemporary preachers, discloses a significant element in the modern mind.

These signs all indicate that the church is face to face with a powerful opponent whom we have come to name " secularism " in preference to the comparatively narrow word " atheism."

The most interesting feature of this development is its effect upon the missionary enterprise.
Indeed the very term " secularism " was coined by
men whose primary interest lay in missions. This
enterprise has been comparatively slow to recognize
the tremendous changes which modern civilization
and the Christian religion have had to undergo. In
1910 the missionary organizations of Protestantism,
meeting at Edinburgh, could still look forward to
a period of great progress in the evangelization of
the world, in view of the ever growing political,
economic and cultural interdependence of all its
units. They did not realize the hostility (or at least
the indifference) to religion of the very forces
which they hoped to engage in advancing their
cause. When the Jerusalem missionary conference
was held eighteen years later, the atmosphere had
changed entirely. One of the most significant
features of the discussion at this meeting was the
consideration given to the problem of secularism.
In consequence, numerous reporters observed with
amazement that the representatives of Christian
missions, who previously had defined their task in
terms of the conversion of non-Christian people to
Christianity, now joined hands with the adherents
of the other great religious cults of the world in

view of the rise of a common enemy, the spirit of secularism. This, if anything, is a clear proof of the fact that religion finds itself today in a state of crisis. It must be noted that this modern crisis affects the whole world of religion and not only the life of a particular historical faith, as was the case in the other crises of Christian history discussed above.

The discovery of the means by which this crisis can be met and perhaps overcome is the most pressing task of contemporary Christians. Before we discuss the various ways suggested to accomplish this task, we must point out that one method often applied to the situation is wholly inadequate, because it is purely negative. This is the method which consciously ignores the fact of crisis and suggests to the church that it continue in its tested course of the past while resolutely refusing to consider the causes and forces which have produced the modern critical conditions. The group which proposes this method has chosen to call itself fundamentalist, suggesting thereby that it still clings, in spite of what our time may demand, to the foundations upon which the church of the past was built, that is to say, to the authorities of Scripture and creeds. It is evident that such an attitude can be adopted only at great cost, at the cost of seclusion from the world.

37

It is remarkable, indeed, that the fundamentalist sections of the church do not appear to be more profoundly disturbed by the fact that the modern world runs along without paying more than slight attention to their voices. On the other hand, the number of Christians who consider themselves members of this group is so remarkably large that it must startle the innocent outsider who, preoccupied with the problems of modern life, is apt to underestimate the number of those who cultivate their Christian traditionalism with a loyalty as curious as it is admirable. But it is certainly neither sane nor wise intentionally to ignore an existing historical fact. For this reason, the fundamentalist method cannot receive serious attention from us when we consider the concrete problem of the contemporary religious crisis.

A discussion of the positive solutions that are offered must concern itself first of all with that movement which claims to take the modern situation most seriously, i.e., with the group which, under the banner of Humanism, was in the limelight a short time ago. The religious Humanists may be said to be the representatives of secularized religion. They do not deny the reality of the spirit of religious devotion. To them it is identical with the recognition of the fact that life is not as it ought to be, particularly in so far as many men are denied the realization of the birthright of human beings, the abundant life. They see religion particularly at work in the endeavor to bring about such changes in the total structure of human existence as will transform this world into one in which everyone may develop a rich and good and happy life. They are persuaded that the content of the historical religions no longer suffices for the quest of the good life. They openly deny the existence of God (or of gods) and therefore abandon all consideration of religious ideas and practices which are dependent on such theistic belief. They desire to concern themselves with the problems of man and his universe as modern science has made them clear. Their chief authority is, therefore, the modern scientific spirit, which they demand should be made the agent of a moral transformation of man. Observing that science has radically changed man's outlook upon life, they proceed to develop a program for the cultivation of human living, built upon the methods and results of the scientific endeavor. The findings of modern biology, anthropology and astronomy enable them to give a new answer to the perennial human question about the origin of life: Man is a link, perhaps the final one, in the long chain of events that composes the evolutionary process which has been going on for millions of years; he must understand himself primarily as a product of nature whose course is now, thanks to the research of the natural sciences, no longer as incomprehensible as it was a few centuries ago. Thus man is told to define his place in life not in terms of himself, as if the universe had been created for his special benefit, but rather in terms of a long natural process, in which, objectively speaking, he plays but an insignificant part. Such a conception, of course, is not meant to depreciate in any way the high value which is to be placed upon human life. It leads, however, to a new interpretation of the purpose of living. As the natural sciences have helped man to understand his place in the totality of the universe, so they have also given him means by which he can adjust himself to the natural processes and by which he may even control them. Scientific technique and the machine are new tools in man's hands which determine his outlook upon life. But only when they are used by a society which is governed by the methods and results of the new social sciences of economics, sociology and psychology will they become useful in the fullest manner. The most urgent immediate task, therefore, is the development of education on the basis of the sciences, both natural and social, for only with their help can society as a whole be taught to construct a life completely in accordance with that knowledge which has become the factor by which our age is distinguished from all preceding periods of history.

The appeal of this program is profound because it is universal. It transcends the limitations imposed upon human groups by their historical traditions. From the point of view of theoretic and practical science, all mankind is united in a new way. The distinctions which now obtain between races and nations and social classes will break down, so one hopes, as scientific education conquers all parts of the earth; and the taboos of religious, racial, national and tribal history will vanish before the enlightening influence of modern science with its universally valid methods. It is this aspect of the scientific world-view which has led to the universal religious crisis and has caused the world-religions to subordinate their rivalries with one another to the requirements of common defense against the spirit which challenges them all alike. The religious radicals whom we, very inadequately, call

Humanists can thus point to a world-wide sympathy with their cause. Nor dare it be forgotten that in the eyes of its promoters and defenders this scientific world-view enables man to answer the three fundamental human questions which, up to this day, have been primarily reserved for religion to answer. Kant formulated the three questions as follows: What can I know? What may I hope for? What shall I do? On the basis of scientific realism, so the claim runs, these questions can now be answered more concretely and often more satisfactorily than was possible with the help of the old religious world-views. The apparent power of this claim is probably the reason why so many of those who have received a scientific education have left the church and why large sections of the so-called cultured middle class in all parts of the world treat organized religion with indifference.

We may now consider the value of the humanistic method of dealing with the religious crisis. Is this the proper way of treating the modern problem of religion? First of all, it is necessary to point out that the concept of religion which underlies this view is very peculiar. One must evaluate it from two points of view. In the first place, it is to be noted that the adherents of Humanism do not wish to be called irreligious. They claim to cultivate a truly religious concern. Religion to them is "the shared quest for a satisfying life." One of their spokesmen [2] declares: "The very vernacular use of the term religion is tending to hasten the identification of religion with the questing process. When a man commits himself to a great cause we say that cause becomes his religion. We speak of men who make their art, or their business, or their social theory, their religion. Communism is said to be the religion of young Russia, as indeed it is." In the second place, they interpret the historical religions of the world in terms of the " social quest to find satisfactory values for all mankind." [3] Ludwig Feuerbach described the essence of religion as a reflection of human desires into a transcendent realm, and proposed therefore to change men " from friends of God to friends of men, from believers to thinkers, from worshipers to workers, from candidates for the ' Yonder ' to students of the ' Here,' from Christians, who, according to their own confession, are partly animals and partly angels, to men, whole men." Much in the same man-

[2] C. W. Reese, *Humanist Religion*. New York, Macmillan, 1931, p. 53.
[3] Ibid., p. 50.

ner modern Humanists interpret all positive religion from an anthropological point of view. The historical religions then appear to be crude and superstitious attempts to attain the good life. While their symbols and beliefs about God and a divine world must now be abandoned, their inner spirit can be carried on.

It is apparent that this definition of religion cannot claim to be factual or objective, but that it is interpretative. To be sure, there is probably no study of the history and the essence of religion which can be called wholly objective. Nevertheless, it can hardly be doubted that the Humanist's understanding of religion ignores that feature in it which gives it its character. It is impossible to hold that religion is to be discovered primarily in its beliefs concerning this world or the next, but it is just as impossible to derive its essence from an analysis of human wants. Or, if we are to give the widest possible interpretation to the definition of the religious life by calling it the quest for the good life, we should surely include in a description of this quest, as it undoubtedly has accompanied man through his history, a reference to man's recognition of those factors and elements in his and nature's life which clearly transcend his or its making and control. It is this aspect of living which allots a very special field to religion and makes it appear as a special and individual phenomenon in human life. And it is this aspect which the radical leaders of religious thought overlook, apparently with intention. The observation which is often made, that the recognition of those factors in life which transcend the control of living beings is primarily due to a state of ignorance which possibly may be surpassed in the future, is not very astute. It ignores the most profound human problem, the problem which is raised by man's awareness of the fact that he is cast into a *given* existence. This problem is perpetuated by his persistent query as to *why* there is existence. It cannot be assumed that the search for the meaning of life will ever end or die. And so long as this search persists to plague the human mind, religion will continue to engage man's central attention. To be sure, one may say that this search will lead men first of all to metaphysical speculation. But it ought to be admitted that metaphysics is never hostile to religion, and that it never has replaced the peculiar air of conviction which marks the religious life. For what is the object of speculation to the metaphysician is the object of reverence and worship to the religious person.

45

That which constitutes existence in its concreteness and in its meaningfulness, that which invests it with what it is and ought to be, is called divine by the religious person. The historical-psychological researches of Rudolf Otto have irrefutably shown that all religious worship devotes itself to this numinous factor of life, recognizing it as a *mysterium tremendum* and as a *mysterium fascinans*.

In view of all this the charge must be made against the radical group of religious leaders, whom we call Humanists, that they have failed to do justice to the fundamental feature in the phenomenon of religion. Therefore, they cannot be expected to make a positive contribution to the task of overcoming the religious crisis. Their whole program — worthy as it is in many, particularly its practical, aspects — fails to do justice to religion itself. What of religion there is left in it, is but a remnant of the thing itself. It is merely the spirit of devotion which is retained. This, however, does not deserve to be called religion in the true sense of the word, since it is not linked to the divine (that is, to that which is worshiped as superhuman, super-worldly, " supernatural "), but merely to a cause or causes proposed by men for the improvement of their station. The metaphysical as well as the

46

truly religious quest for the meaning of life is radically and intentionally denied. This quest must be considered more fundamental than the quest for the " good " life, i.e., the " improved " life, which the Humanists have inscribed upon their banner.

In view of this analysis, it is not surprising that Humanism has not become the challenger of the churches which it promised to be during the short period of its flourishing a few years ago. Its own followers find themselves involved in more problems than they can solve from their strictly humanist viewpoint. The main service which this movement can render is to bring the churches, their leaders and people, face to face with the religious crisis itself. If Humanism does not do justice to religion, it certainly does take seriously what we called the spirit of secularism. As a matter of fact, it has carried this spirit directly into the churches. It must be considered the most concrete representative of the crisis of religion within Christianity itself. If it ever were to prevail, the church as a church would die. Then the crisis would have ended without being overcome.

Another method by which it is hoped to maintain the confidence of the church in itself is presented by Modernism. In many respects, this

47

method is but the further development of the solution offered in the crisis of the eighteenth century. It appears in many different forms, among which two may be distinguished as outstanding. One is primarily philosophical, historical and theological, and the other is chiefly practical. The former is best represented by what is known as modern German theology and the latter by modern American Protestantism. Theological Modernism has the virtue of having made the Christian religion " intellectually respectable." By the application of the methods of historical criticism, it has produced a new understanding of Christianity and of other religions as well. It has shown them to be psychological or experiential expressions of human life, which, in constant interplay with the cultural enterprises of the various groups of mankind, have assumed definite historic forms. Christianity in particular has been interpreted as the religious experience of the peoples of Europe, constantly nourished by the life, teaching and personality of Jesus of Nazareth, and as the dominant force in the unit of Western civilization, holding together its constitutive Hebrew, Græco-Roman and Germanic elements. The chief general lesson of these studies has been the discovery that Christianity

48

survived throughout the ages because it adjusted itself with remarkable ease to the changing demands of the peoples of whose culture it became an inherent part, while it never surrendered the essentials of its faith in Jesus Christ as the revealer of God the Father and the teacher and example of the love of God and fellow men.

In obedience to this principle, derived from historical investigation, modern theology set itself the task of reinterpreting the Christian faith in the light of modern knowledge. Thus it absorbed modern philosophy, history and science. The works of the learned modern theologians since Schleiermacher contain ever changing presentations of the Christian religion which are dominated by the desire to do justice to historical and contemporaneous Christian experience as well as to all phases of modern knowledge. This tremendous labor has had many important results for the church. 1. It led to the rise of the modern Christian scholar. Few academic groups of modern times can boast of having produced so many world-renowned figures of almost universal scholarship as the modern Protestant faculties. 2. It bestowed upon the church also the gift of highly educated and cultured ministers who, profoundly aware of the needs of mod-

ern life, became the proponents of the advancement
of modern civilization and the leaders of many progressive movements in education and social reform.
3. It established beyond doubt the psychological
and historical fact of religious experience in the life
of man. Although the results of the studies in the
psychology and philosophy of religion have not yet
led to unanimous agreement among the scholars,
the present-day knowledge of the place of religion
in human experience is firmer than ever before.
4. In consequence of these findings, the Christian
religion is seen in wider perspective. The changes
it has undergone in its history are generally admitted, and it is recognized that attempted defini-
tions of its essence must be based upon the total
development of the church. But what is still more
important is that, although by some argument the
belief in the absoluteness of Christianity or at least
its inner supremacy is retained, other religions, particularly the great world-religions, are taken seriously. Modern Christian theology depends also
upon its acquaintance with non-Christian religious
experience. Thus its horizon has been broadened,
both theoretically and practically. The most drastic example of the application of this principle is to
be seen in the view of religion which underlies the

recently published report of the Laymen's Appraisal Commission on Missions.[4] In agreement with the opinions of a minority group among the missionaries, it implies the abandonment of the old methods leading to conversion, which are based upon the conviction of Christianity's possession of absolute religious truth. Instead it favors the cultivation of a co-operative exchange of religious experiences and beliefs with a view toward the mutual enrichment of the respective religious groups. The uniqueness of Christianity is firmly maintained and its superiority is at least implicitly presupposed. It must be recognized, however, that in this view the character of uniqueness is assumed also for the non-Christian religions.

So much for *theological* Modernism. As we now turn to *practical* Modernism, which is best represented in American Protestantism, it must be pointed out first of all that it is possible to make only a theoretical distinction between these two types of Modernism. Nineteenth century German theology has exerted a deep influence upon American religious thinking. And if it cannot be said that the effects of American Christianity upon the German church have been equally strong, it must at

[4] *Rethinking Missions.* New York, 1932.

least be admitted that the characteristic movements of the church in this country are not without parallels in Germany. One difference, however, must be taken into account. With a certain reservation, it is the difference between American and European Protestantism. The reservation refers to two facts: First, the place of Great Britain in this picture is not clearly definable, for not only politically and commercially, but also religiously and theologically, it stands in the middle between Europe and America. Second: The transplantation of old-world traits to this continent has not been without effect upon its religious life, particularly in so far as some of the largest American denominations are the direct offspring of European Protestant groups. The difference then is contained in the word "activism" which, during the last decade, has often been used by Europeans in order to indicate where they feel the presence in American Christianity of something strange and unknown to them. It is doubtless correct that, under the influence of the peculiar American cultural climate, the churches here have developed a temper which is altogether lacking in Europe. This is due to many unique facts, of which the following may here be mentioned: the power exerted by New England Puritanism; the separation of church and state which led to the official maintenance of religious tolerance and caused the groups representing the radical wing of Protestantism to seek a future in America; the profound influence of the frontier with its spirit of adventure and virility; the emphasis upon organization which marks the industrial era of American history. Under these various influences modern American Protestantism has assumed a character all its own. Alongside the two old evangelical confessions, Lutheranism and Calvinism, it has arisen as a third group. Its essence lies in its program, which calls for the transformation of society by Christian ethical ideas. The ideal of the establishment of the Kingdom of God on earth is its most characteristic trait. In its pursuit certain great American churches consider themselves to be integral parts of society. With the sense of the special responsibility which religion imposes upon man, they devote themselves more than any other group of past or present Christian history to the cause of a holy society. The will of God begins to be fulfilled, they believe, as an ever increasing number of people identify themselves with the church by becoming its sworn members, thus entering a social group which stands and fights for the assertion of

Christian love in all phases of life. It is the task of the church, so one believes, to establish a collective Christian morality. The church must therefore be willing to keep in close touch with the trends and movements of social life and to raise its voice when these trends need to be directed into the channels of social justice. This duty has been imposed upon American Protestantism particularly during the last generation, when the great teachers and heralds of the so-called social gospel demanded that attention be paid to the unique and pressing problems raised by industrialism. Since that time the aspect which we stress as characteristic of American Protestantism has been especially prominent. But it must not be denied that " activistic " tendencies were present long before.

The consequences of this attitude have lately come clearly to light. In the first place, the leaders of the church have been induced to listen very closely to the social scientists and sociologists, and thus they have adopted programs and ideas of social planning which, worthy as they may be, can often be recognized only with difficulty as the real concern of the church. Movements which foster noble moral causes and which therefore should have the support of the churches have been embraced by them so wholeheartedly that they often appear to be primarily agencies of social reform. Hence their worship-services and other " religious " activities have frequently been transformed as if they were means of upholding the morale of a group in society whose special interest is the maintenance of the ideal and program of the good life in the public affairs of the day. For the same reason church groups were sometimes forced to adopt methods of political strategy in order to enforce their programs or in order to protect themselves from loss and defeat in society's struggle between power and power.

The church has thus come to foster activities which do not appear to belong to its realm. Of course, it is often said that religion ought to affect all phases of human life and that the church must therefore consider no issue of living as outside of its sphere. But if this attitude is carried as far as it often is, so that the specific understanding of religion itself is lost in a feverish activism in the interest of international peace, racial integration, settlement of the urban-rural conflict, industrial arbitration, birth control, sanitation, clean sports, better movies, and so forth, it becomes clear that something is radically wrong with the state of the church of Christ. The second feature of modern American

Protestantism which must be pointed out is the loss of a firm understanding of itself. A survey of modern preaching illustrates this observation. Is it not truly amazing that when religion is distinctly referred to in these sermons it needs elaborate and suggestive interpretation and justification, as if a church should not be able to presuppose thorough understanding of this very thing? But in view of the actual situation it is not astonishing that many ministers and even congregations have strongly felt the temptation to embrace the cause of Humanism.

This survey of the two outstanding types of Modernism enables us to answer the question, what it has to offer to the overcoming of the religious crisis. As in the case of Humanism our answer must largely be negative. Modernism also seems to be too deeply involved in the crisis itself to be in a position to repress it successfully. There are two primary reasons for this judgment:

1. In its desire for openness of mind and for adjustment to the trends and needs of the day, Modernism, both in its theological and practical forms, has intentionally or unconsciously adopted a philosophy and a world-view which are dramatically out of accord with the character of religion and of Christianity in particular. It has permitted

itself to grow into a conformity with the world which does not benefit the Christian religion. It is beset on all sides with the rationalism and moralism of the eighteenth and nineteenth centuries, the truth and urgency of which depend almost entirely upon the doctrine of the autonomy of man. And no religion, and certainly not the Christian religion, can survive if it be understood as the concern of autonomous man. But Modernism has attempted to interpret religion in all its aspects — philosophical, historical, psychological, doctrinal and practical — from the point of view of anthropology. In spite of all its theoretical and practical knowledge of religion, it has lost God. Hence it is drawn into the conflicts of human life to such a degree that it can no longer speak with that authority or objectivity which ought to be expected of those who believe in God. It is this aspect of Modernism which brings it so dangerously close to the heresy of Humanism. But it has never fallen into the pit of this error, because it never permitted itself to doubt the place of the church and religion. And this brings us to the discussion of the second reason why Modernism is helpless in the present crisis of religion.

2. From the very start, Modernism has taken

Christianity for granted. It has always thought and acted on the basis of the existent church. As a matter of fact, its chief purpose was and is a defense of the church. Modernism is an apologetic movement. To be sure, it has been exceedingly critical of the orthodox conceptions, teachings and practices of Christian tradition, but it has never been critical of Christianity or of religion as such. It has always gone back to Jesus, and when a few hypercritical or hypersensitive men nursed doubt as to whether Jesus actually ever existed, they were indignantly vituperated or laughed out of countenance. And it could always point to the church as a healthy and strong institution. But in spite of all this two questions were very persistently raised: What is Christianity? and, What is the church? The answer which Harnack gave with such scholarly confidence and gentlemanly self-assurance has long been deemed insufficient. But the questions persist. And who among the Modernists can be said to have given them a cogent answer? Hence it was possible for the word *quest* to become almost sacred in Christian circles, for the leading Modernist journal to publish an editorial on " The Cult of the Questers," for the Laymen's Appraisal Commission on Missions to suggest that the missionary activity of the church be also made part of the quest for the truth or the true religion.

All this, so it seems, does not furnish Modernism with a proper defense against the crisis of religion which is caused by the widespread doubt that Christianity and religion in general have any valid contribution to offer toward the victory over life's ills and toward the understanding of the process of living in this world. As a matter of fact, the Modernists seem to share this doubt; they themselves do not claim to know the truth!

Hence the Modernists are not good defenders of the church against Humanism; secularism is at their very door and they are not strong enough to battle with it.

To many, who go so far as to agree with the observation that religion finds itself in a state of crisis (and there are, indeed, many who will not even admit the justice of such an observation) a new theological movement, which has attracted the attention of the whole Christian world, appears to be the only savior. It has been claimed that Barthianism is inaugurating a new period of reformation. The various representatives of this theological group by no means agree with one another, but their views are sufficiently alike to warrant a common name. All of them, notably Barth, Brunner and Gogarten, hold the same theological tenets in so far as they are critical of the present religious situation. They took their rise in the camp of the Modernists. Admitting the validity of the criticism which this school directed against orthodoxy, and sharing with it most of its views concerning the interpretation of the Bible and historical tradition, nevertheless they react violently against the constructive efforts of modernist theologians. Instead they offer a new Christian thought, based upon a new appreciation and a rediscovery of the phenomenon of revelation. This new thought is expressed in manifold ways. 1. It leads to the claim that all theology must be theocentric, instead of anthropocentric. In contrast to modernist interpretation, the Christian experience of God is said to depend upon the recognition of a unique and miraculous act of the transcendent God. 2. In consequence, all true theology is understood to be dialectical in so far as all human statements about God and his actions can be but the broken reflections of a being who lives in a light which no one can approach unto. 3. In line with this argument, there is a tendency to introduce a new philosophical approach to theological problems. In contrast to all naturalism, positivism, and especially idealism, the various representatives of Barthianism have sought affiliation with the new philosophical schools of Germany. Bultmann depends upon the metaphysical-phenomenological realism of M. Heidegger, known as *Existentialphilosophie*, Gogarten upon the historical realism of E. Grisebach, the author of the critical work entitled *Gegenwart*, and Brunner, partly under the inspiration of Gogarten, seems to give room to the ethical realism of the famous Jewish philosopher-theologian Martin Buber, author of a philosophical essay entitled *I and Thou*. 4. Only Barth has tried to keep aloof from philosophical entanglement, and has purified his thought in this respect with increasing decision and passion. In the course of time he has made it clear that, from the beginning, his main intention has been directed toward the development of a new biblical theology, based upon the recognition of the unique claim of the Bible that God, who must never be understood in the terms of man, has disclosed himself in Jesus Christ. The Christian church, he declares, is constantly confronted by the Bible and in dependence upon its message proclaims the fact of God's revelation. Theology is conceived as the criticism of the preaching of the church by the one adequate criterion, the Word of God, to which the men of the Bible bear witness. 5. Such a position leads to the condemnation of Modernism as well as of Roman Catholicism on the charge that both have deviated from the true Christian theological task, the former by humanizing the Word of God in the attempt to interpret it by means of man's psychical, social or cultural experience and in terms of the analysis of his existence, the latter by imbedding the absolute Word of God in the channels of a sacramental and hierarchical human institution. 6. This highly critical modern theology is apparently reactionary. It is nourished by an understanding which the church had of itself, before it came in contact with the tendencies of the civilization which we call modern. It favors the thought of the Reformers. Barth in particular seems lately to prefer the genius of Luther to the brilliance of Calvin, upon whom he formerly relied to a great extent. 7. Most striking is the Barthian thesis, that the world of history and science, the whole world of modern culture, recognition of which forced theology into a new course, is not of positive theological significance. Barth himself does not even allude to these significant problems, and he appears to be critical of Brunner's effort to demonstrate the sufficiency of Christian thought by a critical analysis of the various types of modern thought and action. Gogarten is primarily interested in the problems of history, but he is incapable of appreciating it as a process. In consequence, the charge has often been made against the Barthians that they neglect the ethical problem. They have felt the justice of such a criticism. Gogarten was the first to offer a corrective by attempting to restore an ethics of authority. Brunner has recently published a monumental work on ethics which takes full recognition of the concrete problems of living. It may mark a change in his whole outlook, a change which is suggested by his declared intention of applying the Christian insight of the Reformers to contemporary forms of life. Thus his work seems to tend toward the restoration of a Protestant theological traditionalism, which, it may be remarked, has enjoyed continued cultivation both in the Lutheran and Reformed churches throughout the modern centuries, more or less undisturbed by the spirit of modern times. A similar tendency is to be noted with respect to Barth. It would not be surprising in these circumstances if the total effect of Barthianism would ultimately lead to a restoration of confessional Protestant theology.

With this observation we have suggested the chief reason why Barthianism cannot be productively helpful in the modern religious crisis. The cure which it advises is that the church return to itself, after it has identified itself under modernist leadership with the world to such a degree that it has almost reached the abyss of self-defeat. But the question is whether such a cure is possible. The church is challenged by the widespread query whether its dependence upon God and its cultivation of religious knowledge and action is not superfluous. The Barthians recognize this question. They admit its justice and even go so far as to agree with the modern critics of religion. They too propagate a criticism of religion, not from the point of view of secularism, but from the point of view of God. They declare that they are not concerned with religion, but with revelation, not with man's ideas and experiences of God, but with God's doings with man. They are not interested in worship of any kind, but in man's recognition of God who has revealed himself in Jesus Christ.

In other words, they make the unique claim that what is offered as the modern understanding of religion is indeed not worthy to be preserved, because it implies a betrayal of the Christian message of God's revelation. It cannot be doubted that the Barthians have won a strong following with this criticism. The Christian church is indeed still an active reality. Instead of taking this fact simply for granted, as the Modernists do, the Barthians take it very seriously, especially in so far as the church is constantly confronted by the Bible. While the Humanists propose to solve the problem of the religious crisis by allowing only a religion which completely identifies itself with the spirit of secularism, and while the Modernists rely primarily upon the actuality and presence of the religious life, the Barthians wish to depend almost exclusively upon the Bible and on a church which recognizes the special worth of the Bible. But since they cannot go back behind the secularism which dominates the modern world nor behind the wider knowledge of religions which characterizes the modern religious consciousness, they find themselves facing most difficult problems, when they attempt to recover the absoluteness of the Bible and the revelation of which it speaks. Indeed, the Barthian conception of revelation and the word of God is by no means clear. It is so deeply enveloped in theological sophistry and dialectics that it is the subject primarily of academic theological argument and cannot be made effective among the people, to whom it appeals chiefly emotionally as a repristination of Christian conservatism.

One fact, however, is perfectly clear, whatever the reactions to the Barthian theology as theology may be: It has been a powerful influence upon the religious life of our time, because it teaches us to take God seriously in his divinity. It impresses us with the realization that when we use the word "God," we refer to an aspect of reality which transcends us and our creativity as well as our control, and which, if we are compelled to translate it into life, shatters the self-sufficiency of any form. In other words, Barth and his friends have led us to recover the sense of true religious devotion which is directed toward a life based upon a foundation which transcends human or worldly creation, and which springs from the awareness that the meaning of life is a first principle that must be recognized before it can be gained.

In so far as this is true, Barthianism indicates the way in which the crisis of religion may be overcome. This way may be described in old words by the sentence: " God is in heaven and man is on earth and man cannot live on earth unless he recognizes the heaven above it." Or it may be suggested in philosophical language by saying that life is meaningful only if it is qualified by theonomous rather than by autonomous decisions and judgments.

Wherever such lives are lived, the religious crisis does not exist. Since we can be sure of the actuality of many such lives in all circles and groups of men everywhere, it may be that we should not allow the crisis to frighten us. Nevertheless, it is a fact, and a vast majority of our contemporaries cry for guidance. This can be provided only by new thought. That is why we have to concern ourselves with the analysis of the crisis and the means of overcoming it.

In this connection we must mention a movement which has lately swept the West, claiming that it can give disillusioned men a new religious life. It is the Oxford Movement or Buchmanism. By the revival of religious emotions, by surrender to God, by commitment to an unselfish life of honesty, purity, unselfishness and love, by a renewal of the practice of confession and by the sharing of religious experiences, by reliance upon divine guidance and by a revivification of first-century immediacy and spirituality, it proposes, and claims to

67

solve, the problems of the religious crisis in a practical manner.

It must be pointed out that by such means the
solution of the problem is merely anticipated in
the emotions — which is to say that, in reality,
it is postponed. For we cannot doubt the fact
that Western civilization is today in a state of
transition. More particularly, we should say that
the doctrine of the autonomy of man which theoretically and practically has upheld the last phase of
this civilization is now found wanting. What the
ultimate effect of this breakup will be, no one can
yet suggest with certainty. But it is evident that the
realization of the inadequacy of a life dominated
by the spirit of human self-determination is of great
religious importance. This realization has already
entered all fields of human endeavor. In this respect, our age is a religious period. The time is
again fulfilled. It is our duty to know this and to
be patient. Only by a comprehension of the
changes which are befalling us can we be sufficiently prepared for a new religious certainty.

The considerations of these pages are intended
to further the understanding of the situation in
which we find ourselves. They do not offer a
solution of the problem to which they are ad-

dressed. But they hint at the solution in so far as they contain the observation that an age which has attained more power of world control than any other longs for sanctification by a new sense of God. The spirit of secularism has brought about the crisis of the old and of contemporary religion. A new religious sense, built upon a new certainty of God, must bring the spirit of secularism into a crisis. When this event occurs, we shall be saved. Perhaps the time is not far distant when a prophet will arise among us who, fully imbued with the mood and spirit of our era, will speak to us in the name of the living God with such power and authority that all who long for salvation will be compelled to listen. In the meantime, we must learn to be humble in the awareness that it is God, the Lord of all life, who has laid his hand upon us in this crisis. And we must learn to pray: We believe, O Lord, help thou our unbelief. He who will have authority to declare that this prayer has been heard will be the leader of the movement by which the crisis will be overcome.

PART TWO

By Francis P. Miller

AMERICAN PROTESTANTISM AND THE
CHRISTIAN FAITH

IN every part of the world the Protestant movement finds itself beleaguered by the forces of
militant nationalism — a nationalism which represents for the most part an utter denial of the Christian faith. The precariousness of the position of
the Protestant churches consists in the fact that
the nature of nationalism is such that it can isolate
sections of the Protestant community and destroy
these sections in detail. Though the destruction
of the universal elements in the Protestant faith has
progressed further in certain sections of the German church than anywhere else this same process
is actively present in American life. An environment favorable to this process has been created by
some of our foremost educators, philosophers and
theologians. It has been created by men who are
quite unconscious of the indirect consequences of
their intellectual assumptions, and who as individuals would energetically oppose the extension of
the authority of national culture over the whole
range of life. Yet such an extension is actually
taking place as a result of the religious attitudes

which these men have adopted, and as this extension takes place it carries with it a mortal threat to the integrity of the Christian faith. This situation obviously requires the immediate attention of those who have at heart the future of the American Protestant churches.

I

CHRISTIAN FAITH AND HUMAN CULTURE

Very definite assumptions lie behind the argument of this chapter. These assumptions will be accepted by some and rejected by others. The examination of their validity is the responsibility of the theologian and the church historian, but their acceptance is in the last analysis a matter of faith. To men who live under the authority of the historic Christian tradition their validity is self-evident. My intention is not to attempt to prove that they are true, but to assert the consequences of their truth. Some of these assumptions are:

1. That the object of the Christian faith is a Reality which has an existence of its own and is not to be identified with your existence or my existence

or with the world or universe in which you and I live and move and have our being.

2. That that Reality is the Creator of all things visible and invisible and that his relation to you and me and to the world in which you and I live and move and have our being is the relation of the " Maker " to the thing " being made." Man has not made God in his image, but God has made man in his image. Man is the creature; God is the Creator.

3. That man as creature has sufficient freedom to accept or reject the purposes of his Creator, but not sufficient freedom to escape from the consequences of acceptance or rejection.

4. That the character of God the Creator is disclosed in the divine drama of the life, death and resurrection of Jesus Christ.

5. That the community of men and women who share this faith and attempt to live this life constitutes the unique medium in each age for the continued disclosure of God's creative and redemptive purposes.

6. That it is the business of this community of faith — the Church Universal — in our time and in every time to declare God's judgment and to witness to his love.

7. That the actualities of history — the concrete events of the contemporary scene — are a record of the life-giving power of the love of God and of the death-bringing consequences of man's denial of that love.

When the word "Christian" is used in the following pages it is used to define the religion characterized by the above assumptions. Granting that this is an accurate use of the word "Christian," one deduction may immediately be drawn, and that is that the Christian religion is in its essence a universal religion. It is a religion equally good and true for all men, everywhere and in all times. The Christian cross is not an American cross or a German cross or a British cross or an Italian cross. It is the possession of any man of any race who understands its message and lives by faith in its transforming power. The reality which that cross reveals is not the by-product of a particular national culture or of a particular racial experience. On the contrary, that reality is utterly independent of the evolution or destiny of particular nations or races. These human collectivities cannot by any virtue or wisdom of their own add one iota to the validity of its truth or subtract one iota from that validity. All a nation or a race can do is to live by that truth

76

or reject it, and in either case the consequences of the choice must be borne.

This is not to say that the form through which the meaning of the Christian cross is interpreted or the form through which its truth is incarnated in the life of any age is not conditioned by the culture of that age. On the contrary, that form will be profoundly influenced by the character of the prevailing culture. It is the content of faith and not the form of its expression which is independent of the character of changing human society.

This distinction between content and form is extremely important, and failure to make such a distinction will lead to the very perversion of truth itself. The reality symbolized by the cross is obviously a part of the content of the Christian faith. " For God so loved the world that he gave his only begotten son . . ." " Except a grain of wheat fall into the ground and die, it abideth by itself alone but if it die it bringeth forth much fruit." The fact of God's love is disclosed on the cross; the truth that life is only generated by the self-less laying down of life — these are eternal and universal ingredients of the Christian faith. They are not logical deductions from special systems of thought. They are not the product of men's imagination. They are not individual attitudes or social values peculiar to this or that society or this or that culture. They are no more European than they are Asiatic — no more American than they are African. On the contrary, they are a part of the grain of the universe as God has created it. They constitute elements of that ultimate structure of life — the realm of God — with which we have to do every moment of our lives.

The content of the Christian faith is not made by man. It is given to man. It is given by the reality of the realm of God. That realm exists in its own right. Man cannot call it into being or dissolve it at his pleasure. It is the one and only reality whose universal presence can be assumed in advance. There is no place in all the cosmos to which man can go where he will not find the realm of God waiting for him. It is there — and to be alive means to be doing something about it. Man is either continually associating himself with its creative purposes or continually dissociating himself from them. And whether he is doing the one or the other is the decisive fact of his existence. For within the limits which the realm of God defines there is eternal life; beyond those limits there is death.

The content of the Christian faith is supplied by the character of God and the nature of his world. The Christian does not invent that content any more than the scientist invents the content of what he calls the laws of science. The scientist as scientist and the scientist as Christian is doing exactly the same thing — describing a *given* structure of reality whose existence is in no sense dependent upon his imagination or his ideals. The methods used to verify belief in the structure of the realm of God and in the structure of the created world as defined by science are different, but neither of these structures can be discovered except by men who humbly stand in the presence of *that which is*. It is the responsibility of the man of faith to describe the structure of the realm of God, just as it is the responsibility of the scientist to describe the structure of the created world.

The description of the man of faith, however, will never be as satisfactory as the description of the man of science. This is due to the nature of man himself, as well as to the difference between the nature of the realm of God and the nature of the world science describes. Man's nature is such that he can never quite put his finger on the realm of God — the best of men grope toward it without ever really grasping it, while the same good men as scientists can more or less take the world of science within their grasp. The most accurate statement the man of faith can make will still be incomplete and imperfect because his statement is a reflection of his own imperfection — a relative being who even in his most exalted moments is tainted with sin and whose comprehension is constantly being warped by his slight intelligence and small faith. Imperfect as the statement of the man of faith may be, the reality about which his statement is made remains entirely independent of that imperfection.

The content of faith is independent, but the form through which faith is expressed is not independent. The word " form " is used to describe the medium through which the content of truth is communicated. It includes language, ritual, and activity of all kinds which are intended to symbolize or implement truth. The form is of course in part determined by the character of the eternal reality which it symbolizes and to which it witnesses. But it is also in part determined by the concrete time-space situation in which the witness is given. The adequacy of the form will depend upon the degree of its success in articulating eternal truth in terms comprehensible to any given generation or society. Hence appropriate forms will always be dynamic and changing. A static form is sure to be a false symbol. On the other hand, the limits of change are narrow. They are definitely fixed by the nature of the reality which is being symbolized. It is the business of men of faith to see to it that they employ the forms which, in a particular cultural environment, will give the clearest and most exact description of the content of their faith to the people who live in that environment. Consequently the choice of form is important, and rightly deserves continual attention.

But the moment form takes precedence over content religious faith begins to expire. And if preoccupation with form becomes so complete that it results in form being mistaken for content, then faith is already dead. This happened on a wide scale in Europe during the latter part of the fifteenth century, and produced the Protestant Reformation. It is happening on a wide scale now. There is a striking contrast, however, between the circumstances which gave rise to this phenomenon in the fifteenth century, and the circumstances which have given rise to it at the present time. The most ironical feature of the present situation is that Protestants now find themselves in exactly the same position as the Catholics were four hundred years ago. The society of the pro- testers has in the fulness of time succumbed to the same historic fate as that which formerly overtook those against whom they protested. In the early fifteenth century the Catholics mistook static ec- clesiastic forms for the content of their faith. In the early twentieth century Protestants are mis- taking dynamic cultural forms for the content of their faith. And the triumph of cultural forms over religious content is even more deadly than the triumph of ecclesiastic forms. For even when the use of ecclesiastic forms is perfectly meaning- less and hypocritical these forms still refer back to a religious truth once understood and appro- priated. And the day comes when men begin to wonder again *what* it was that the forms were origi- nally intended to symbolize. As they allow their curiosity to explore this and that hypothesis they rediscover the long-forgotten truth, and in that re- discovery faith is born again.

Cultural forms, on the other hand, can never be relied upon to refer back to a tradition of re- ligious truth. Culture as a social phenomenon is far more extensive and inclusive than the Christian faith. Wherever a living faith exists culture will be profoundly modified by that faith, but culture from its very nature will always include some elements which are hostile to faith. There are strands of culture which will lead toward the church and there are others which will lead away from the church. Cultural forms are signposts pointing back to stages in the total social evolution of a particular people or nation. Consequently when in the life of the church cultural forms triumph over religious content and faith disappears, and when in the course of time men begin to wonder what content these forms were originally intended to symbolize, the historic explanations which they will advance will be given in terms of national or racial destiny rather than in terms of a rediscovered religious truth. The cultural signposts will point backward, but not to the cross. The German swastika has been planted in many a church of the German Christians, but for the historians of this period it will serve as a reference point to Adolf Hitler and not to Jesus Christ.

II

CAN THE PROTESTANT CHURCHES SURVIVE AS RELIABLE WITNESSES TO CHRISTIAN FAITH?

Having won their liberty from enslavement to the Roman hierarchy, Protestants are now in process of being enslaved by their respective national cultures and it remains to be seen whether their last estate may not be worse than their first. All over the Protestant world it is obvious that preoccupation with the cultural form in which their faith is expressed is a more decisive factor in determining the future of the Protestant churches than preoccupation with the content of their faith. If this trend continues the issue before the Protestant churches is clear: Are the different Protestant communities to become the spiritual or ethical facets of their respective national cultures, thereby ceasing to be Christian, or will they survive as reliable witnesses to the Christian faith? If they are to survive as reliable witnesses, what conditions of survival have to be fulfilled?

The question is not, of course, being raised as to the survival of Protestant institutions in one form

84

or another. Even if the Protestant denominations lost all semblance of their Christian origins they would continue to exist for generations and possibly for centuries as societies concerned with the ethical life or as societies responsible for maintaining national morale. The organization of the Protestant community will certainly survive, but the question is, "Survive for what?" Can the Protestant churches survive as *reliable witnesses* of the Christian faith?

If the assumptions which lie behind this chapter are sound, a *reliable witness* would mean a witness to truths which are recognized by men of faith in all lands and in all ages and under all circumstances as being equally valid for them and for their fellows. In other words, the frame of reference to which the witness would refer would be a universally acknowledged one. Men would speak as Americans or Germans or Chinese but their frame of reference would not be the culture of their respective nations. In so far as they spoke as Christians their frame of reference would be that of Christendom. What is Christendom? It is the earthly counterpart of that reality which St. Augustine called the City of God. The City of God is both in the world and beyond the world. It extends from eternity into time. It is *there*, but it is also *here*. And we call that portion of the City which confronts us in the here and now, Christendom. Hope in Christendom is the hope of the world. Without that hope there is no hope. Apart from Christendom the world is the madhouse described so accurately each morning in the daily press.

How far is Christendom the frame of reference for Protestants? To put such a question is to answer it. But it would be an injustice to the Protestant tradition to leave the answer without an explanation.

For in the great days of the Protestant movement the Protestant churches lived within the framework of Christendom. That was a gift which they had received from Rome. The sense of Christendom had been so indelibly traced on men's minds that they were quite unconscious of the extent to which they owed it to their social heritage. It seemed to them to be a part of the order of things like the starry vault of heaven above. Protestant leaders of the sixteenth century were unaware of the fact that primitive European man not only did not naturally possess the sense of Christendom but that Christendom was the complete antithesis of life as the primitive European knew it — the complete antithesis of his devotion to tribalism and his passion for piracy. During many generations under the tutelage of the Catholic church his piratical nature was slowly transformed and his tribalism was gradually sublimated. In other words, the consciousness of Christendom, in so far as that existed, was an acquired consciousness. It had been acquired through the teaching and example of the medieval church. Since it had been acquired it could also be lost. It would be lost as soon as the framework of thought and life disappeared upon which it had grown through the centuries. Christians could destroy this framework either by ignoring its essential features or by ceasing to use it as a frame of reference. This is what actually happened.

Though the Catholic church itself eventually failed to realize the truth of its own teaching it had done its job so well that for three centuries after the Reformation Catholic, Protestant and freethinker alike continued to live under the spell of Christendom. During the Enlightenment the concept of Christendom degenerated into the concept of a cosmopolitan European culture, but even this bastard offspring was powerful enough to restrain the violence of perverted nationalism. It was only a century ago, and in Germany, that one of the greatest minds of the age could hospitably entertain his nation's conqueror and do so with evident satisfaction. The suggestion that he might betray Germany by cultivating the friendship of Napoleon would have seemed to Goethe the sheerest stupidity, and he would have been dumbfounded by the prospect that the stupidity of his own age would be the wisdom of the next.

During the three centuries when European Protestants continued to live more or less within the framework of Christendom the Protestant communities continued to be characterized by a certain measure of universality in their life and thought. This relative universality was derived from two sources:

1. It was derived from the common value attached to the Bible by nearly all of the Protestant churches.

2. And it was further derived from the fact that all of the Protestant churches were rooted in the soil of a common culture — the culture of Western Europe.[1]

[1] This latter fact is seldom considered by the apologists of Protestantism. Yet its consequences for the Protestant movement have been profound. So long as Protestantism was a European phenomenon it wore a mask of apparent universality derived from

88

If the Bible and Western European culture were the most important sources of such universality as Protestantism possessed, it is obvious that the time has long since passed when either of these sources could be relied upon to continue to supply Protestants with a universal frame of reference. This fact constitutes the supreme crisis upon which the Protestant movement is now entering. The Protestant churches no longer have a common ground of unity. Since they no longer have a common ground of unity they do not teach truths which are equally valid for all men everywhere, and as long as they do not teach such truths they cannot be regarded as reliable witnesses to the Christian faith.

Some Protestant leaders apparently hope that the Bible may once more prove to be an adequate rallying point. Great as the value of the Bible is, it is inconceivable that it can ever again provide Protestantism with the universal frame of reference which the reliable witness needs.

---

its cultural background. A Dutch Protestant and a Swiss Protestant and a Scotch Protestant could all understand one another tolerably well because they were all inheritors of the same cultural traditions. The perpetuation of this happy situation, however, depended upon the survival of a common culture throughout Western Europe and the permanent confinement of Protestantism within the orbit of that culture. Neither of these conditions was fulfilled.

Other Protestant leaders put their trust in culture rather than in the Bible. They look forward to a new world culture [2] which is to supply the required universal frame of reference.

The proponents of this position would be the first to point out that the culture of Western Europe is no longer capable of serving as the ground of universality. The Protestant churches have moved out into areas of culture which have little or nothing in common with the culture of Western Europe. This has happened through the migrations of peoples from Europe as well as through the work of missionaries. The emerging culture of North America is as different from the culture of Europe as both of these are different in turn from the cultures of the Far East. And this fact alone has enormously increased the difficulty of communication between different branches of the Protestant world.

Those, however, who hope for unity through culture regard this diversity between cultures as a transitional phase preceding the development of a world culture which will result from cross-fertilization between national or racial cultures. The ques-

[2] See *Christian Missions and a New World Culture*, by Archibald G. Baker, Willett, Clark & Company, Chicago; and *Rethinking Missions — a Laymen's Inquiry*, Harper & Brothers, New York.

tion whether or not in the remote future a common world culture will emerge is one which may interest the schools of the prophets but is perfectly irrelevant otherwise. For as far as this century is concerned and the centuries which immediately follow, the answer to that question is perfectly plain. No world culture is emerging or will emerge. The theorists who have constructed this beautiful dream are the contemporary equivalents of those who preached progress before 1914. No more fantastic peg on which to hang the future of Christianity was ever invented by the human imagination. It would not deserve serious consideration if it were not associated with the names of eminent Protestant leaders.

The plain fact is that not only is no world culture emerging but that the trend of events is in exactly the opposite direction. The passions and ambitions of mutually hostile collectivities and not the common interests of a developing world culture are the forces which dominate the age in which we live. All over the world it is the destiny of the nation which is setting the pace for the human caravan. The self-centered nation-state living in fear and jealousy of its neighbors is the force which is conditioning contemporary history. In the presence of this force, belief in an emerging world culture seems like an idle dream spun by men whose monastic seclusion has hidden from them the stark realities of the outer world. Not only is present-day culture not serving as a binding force between nations, but it is being used to accentuate their mutual dissimilarities and animosities. So violent and determined are the different nations that they have captured culture and are busily engaged in prostituting it for their own divisive purposes. This exploitation of culture by the nation-state is the decisive fact of the world in which we live. To belittle that fact is to distort actuality. To ignore it is to become a blind guide for the blind.

It is of course true that there is a world-wide trend toward the employment of an identical industrial technique. No doubt those who think they see an emerging world culture have been impressed by the spread of a common system of industrial production. As a result they have mistaken the generalization of production techniques for a generalization of culture. Their defense would be that the means of production are in the last analysis the decisive factor in determining men's habits and customs. This is the faith of our age. It is a faith common to both capitalists and communists and to the prolific breed of ideologists begotten by our machine civilization. It is a false faith. The mind and spirit of man and not the technique of production he employs eventually determine the form of his society and of his culture.

How is one to account otherwise for the type of social evolution which has taken place during the past century in nations like Germany, France, Great Britain, Russia, Japan and the United States? For several generations the nations of Western Europe have employed what can only be called, in spite of minor variations, a common industrial technique. Have men been bound together by the common use of identical methods of production? On the contrary, during this very same period the peoples have drifted steadily apart, because they wanted different things. It is man who is the source of desire, and not the machine. The same machines are used everywhere but men use the machines for mutually irreconcilable purposes. It is the Nazi movement and not industrial technique which is molding the future of Germany. And the Nazi movement represents a cultural development which utterly contradicts the cultural traditions of Great Britain and France.

Japan and Russia have, during the past twenty

years, moved with breath-taking speed toward the employment of a common industrial technique. But they have not been bound together. The decisive thing about Russia and Japan is that the future of each country is being determined by a totally different set of forces. It is General Araki's cult of Kodo that is molding the future of Japan, and that cultural development is a complete contradiction of recent cultural developments in Russia. It is even more alien to the cultural tradition of the United States.

The march of events is, at least in this field, perfectly plain. The inescapable conclusion to which one is driven by observing it is that the national ethos is far more powerful in determining the shape of things to come than any possible combination of social forces resulting from the appearance of a common world technical civilization. And culture has become the willing slave of the national ethos.

This is the kind of world in which the Protestant church finds itself. To say that its position in that world is precarious is to put the matter mildly. For the Protestant community is without a universal frame of reference. Within the Protestant fold there are of course many individual claims to the possession of a universal frame of reference. But when examined these claims have no justification in the corporate life of the community. That community no longer finds the unity of its message in the common value which it attaches to the Bible. It can no longer rely upon the fact that it originally grew out of the soil of a common Western European culture to ensure comprehension between its different parts. For the culture of Europe has not only not become a world culture, but even in Europe it has been irrevocably broken into bits by the impact of national cultures. Confidence in the emergence of a new world culture to perform the function of supplying Protestants with the same kind of unity which they once derived from Western European culture is a vain and illusory hope.

Without a universal frame of reference of its own and without the hope that world civilization will supply it with such a frame of reference, Protestantism stands exposed and defenseless before the onslaughts of national cultures. If it remains in this position the result is a foregone conclusion. The result will be that the Protestant faith will be destroyed in detail by these different cultures. This destruction is not a matter of prophecy. We are already witnesses of the first stages of the process of destruction. As the process continues Protestantism will tend more and more to lose its sense of universal mission as well as its sense of responsibility for witnessing to the universal truths of the Christian faith. Instead of expiring in courageous resistance, it will save itself by domesticating itself within the different national cultures, and as it does this it will degenerate into a spiritual or ethical manifestation of particular cultures and cease to be a reliable witness to the revelation of God in Christ.

There is no doubt in my own mind that the process of the domestication of Protestantism within national cultures is steadily taking place. This is illustrated by the increasing difficulty which Protestants from different continents, or even from different countries on the same continent, experience in communicating with each other. Ability to speak three or four of the most prevalent languages is not much help, for the barrier to understanding is far more serious than the barrier of language. The barrier consists in the fact that each person tends to articulate his religious experience in terms of his own cultural background. Each continues, of course, to console himself with the delusion that his special system of theology or his particular interpretation of the meaning of the Word of God constitutes a universal frame of reference within which the other person is or ought to be included and that consequently communication between them ought to be possible. But in so far as the actual frames of reference for both are their respective national cultures, the possibility of comprehending each other is not only greatly reduced but may even be rendered nil.

Over a period of more than twenty years I have observed this trend in the life of the Protestant student movements affiliated with the World's Student Christian Federation. The student mind is a very interesting mirror of dynamic social currents. It cannot always be relied upon for accurate interpretation of the present, but as a hint to the future it deserves serious attention. And in the Protestant student world we have more than a hint of what the future holds in store for the churches.

The fact is that some of the barriers which national cultures have imposed upon religious comprehension have already grown so high that very little if any understanding exists across them. To cite the barrier which exists between German Protestant students and American Protestant students may not seem convincing to those who have accustomed themselves to take that barrier for granted. On the other hand, to take it for granted is to admit that a situation exists in which two of the most important branches of the Protestant church no longer possess a common frame of reference. There are of course a few individual exceptions of men and women who by faith have transcended the limitations of their respective German and American churches and have entered as persons into the fellowship of the universal community of faith. These persons are evidence of the power of the love of God which can operate even when denied a corporate home. But such individual exceptions only emphasize more vividly the plight of the church as a whole, as it continues to domesticate itself within the national cultures.

An even more striking evidence of the prevalence of this trend is the increasing lack of comprehension between British and American Protestant students. Here are students who speak the same language and who in many instances share the same political and social traditions. Yet there is almost no communication between them in the realm of faith. There is a good bit of going to and fro across the Atlantic in the interest of sport, and in the interest of education, but there is practically none in the interest of the Christian religion. The one notable exception is the Buchman movement, but its exaggerated pietistic character deprives it of any particular significance as far as the total life of the Protestant churches is concerned. The cessation of significant Christian intercourse between the American and British universities has not been accepted with resignation by those who observed its coming. On the contrary, during the decade after the World War heroic efforts were made to maintain intercourse by organizational devices of one kind and another. These proved entirely ineffective to arrest the trend.

It gives one pause to contrast the present incapacity of British and American Protestant students to communicate with each other with the kind of relationship which prevailed between them fifty years ago. At that time the interflow of life was fairly continuous and had profound consequences for the church on both sides of the Atlantic. The Moody missions to Cambridge and Oxford, and the visits to the United States of the Cambridge Seven or of Henry Drummond were religious events of first-rate importance. In other words, people not only understood each other across the Atlantic but they were able to help each other. Now we no longer seem to understand, and consequently we cannot help.

This disappearance of creative communication between British and American students is merely an extreme instance of a world-wide trend. As Protestant thought domesticates itself within the national cultures, individual Protestants find that their religious language is increasingly incapable of transmitting the meaning of their faith to men of other countries. There is no universal frame of reference which provides a common pattern of thought to the whole Protestant community. Consequently the degradation of Protestantism proceeds apace. This degradation has occurred in the United States as much as in any Protestant land.

III

Is American Religion Christian?

It has been customary in the past for American Protestants to assume the reliability and integrity of their own witness to the Christian faith. There are, of course, bitter family quarrels within the community, but when American Protestantism itself is called in question both fundamentalists and modernists instantly forget their differences and rally to its defense. The liberals may be dismissed with contempt by the realists, the agrarian fundamentalists may be ignored by their up-to-the-minute cosmopolitan brethren, but all alike assume the stability of the foundations of Protestantism. Where doubt is cast upon these foundations it is never directed toward the American section, but is almost invariably directed toward the European section.

The plight of the Protestant churches in Germany is certainly desperate enough to justify all the concern that can be expressed, though one would hope that admiration for the courage of the opposition clergy would exceed consternation at the policy adopted by the " German Christians." But the preoccupation of the leaders of the American churches with the crumbling foundations of European churches seems somewhat gratuitous when the foundations of their own churches are crumbling under their very feet for exactly the same reasons. It would be a salutary act of self-denial on the part of some of our intellectuals if they would resolve for a time to forget the predicament of Protestants overseas and concentrate upon the perilous condition of Protestants in the United States.

The plain fact is that the domestication of the Protestant community in the United States within the framework of the national culture has progressed as far as in any western land. The degradation of the American Protestant church is as complete as the degradation of any other national Protestant church. The process of degradation has been more subtle and inconspicuous, but equally devastating in its consequences for faith.

This is due in part to the fact that the character of our national culture and the traditions of American Protestantism have made them both peculiarly susceptible to fusion. A process which began with a culture molded by religious faith has ended with a religious faith molded by a national culture. Our national culture is the sum total not only of the hopes and desires which our fathers brought with them from Europe but also of their experiences and the experiences of their descendants in conquering and consolidating a continent. And the traditions born out of the experience of creating a new world have in the end proved far stronger than the traditions which were brought from the old world.

American national culture is still in process of formation. It is immature but very dynamic. The environment which it has created is favorable to the development of a technological civilization, but rather unfavorable to the maintenance of the Christian faith. It is therefore natural that religious minds immersed exclusively in that culture should occupy themselves with the construction of a religion better suited than the historic Christian faith to the conservation and promotion of the values of that culture. Sometimes this effort is made from within the church under the name of Christianity. Sometimes it is made from without the church by men consciously emancipated from the Christian tradition. In either case the effect is the same — to lay the foundations of a religion or of a religious attitude which is American rather than Christian, national rather than universal.

This natural national religion which is emerging out of American culture expresses the most characteristic ethical and spiritual aspects of that culture. It is empirical in its approach to religious truth. It sets great store upon human ideals and human values. It is profoundly concerned with the realization of these ideals and values in social relations. It is essentially humanitarian in its outlook on life. It is the champion of personality. And it has a vivid sense of world mission.

In other words the American religion which is developing before our eyes is an expression of many of the qualities of which we are most proud in our national heritage. Its distant roots are of course in the Christian ethic. That is what gives it its plausible façade. That is also what lends such subtlety to its propaganda. If it were an avowedly national cult like General Araki's Kodo in Japan or General Ludendorff's new paganism in Germany, the issue between it and Christianity would be perfectly clear. But since our particular variety of national religion usually employs terms identical with those of the Christian ethic and even with the faith itself, the issue is extremely confused. The test by which the American Protestant church must be finally judged is whether its frame of reference is our national culture or the reality of Christendom. Does the faith to which this church is committed deal with a reality that is universal, true and good for all men everywhere and in all time, or is its faith rather the expression of the highest spiritual insights of our particular American culture? Let there be no mistake about it, these two alternatives are not just different ways of saying the same thing. They are not two facets of the same truth. On the contrary they are diametrically opposite positions. To maintain one means to abandon the other.

It is manifestly unfair to speak of Protestant Christianity in America as if it represented a uniform type of religious faith. And yet when the infinite variety of American Protestantism has been fully recognized — its variety in historic backgrounds, in class affiliations, in creeds and in institutions — the fact remains that what it has in common is perhaps even more impressive than its variety. Viewed from any other part of the world the differentiations between denominations which seem sharp enough in North America tend to fade away or, rather, are overshadowed by the family resemblances which bind the bulk of American Protestants together into a well-defined type as contrasted with Christian communities on other continents.

Within this well-defined American Protestant community there are, as might be expected, various dynamic trends — intellectual and social trends, ethical trends and theological. These give to the Protestant community as a whole its most distinctive characteristics. They reveal the sources of its spiritual vitality, they indicate the decisive interests which motivate it and they provide clues to its future development.

There are, of course, sections of the Protestant church in the United States which are relatively immune to the influences of our evolving national religion. On the other hand, some of the dynamic trends which exert the widest influence over the thought and life of many of the churches have been profoundly influenced by that religion. It is this situation which constitutes a danger for the church as a whole.

The high priest of the movement which is preparing the way in the United States for a national religion as opposed to the Christian religion is Professor John Dewey. As our greatest educator and one of our greatest philosophers he has had an enormous influence on contemporary thought. Professor Dewey himself would be horrified at the suggestion that he is playing into the hands of nationalist forces. He is the outstanding liberal of his generation, a man wholly devoted to the application of ideals to life, and continuously preoccupied with serving the commonweal. Yet both his philosophy and his religion have laid substantial foundations for the American equivalent of the Nazi religion in Germany. The liberals in Germany unwittingly performed this function there. They are performing the same function here. Why? Because their ultimate frame of reference is not a universal faith but national culture.

This is made perfectly plain in Professor Dewey's recent book, *A Common Faith*. In it he discusses the religious attitude toward life which he has adopted for himself. He describes this faith in part " as the unification of the self through allegiance to inclusive ideal ends which imagination presents to us." The crucial question is, what is the imagination? For Professor Dewey the imagination is obviously the organ of faith. It serves the same function for him that " conscience " does for the Puritan, or the Pope does for the Catholic. It is a humanist's equivalent for the authority which the theist finds in God. On the basis of the enlightened and informed imagination, Professor Dewey hopes to build his universal community of those who have a common religious attitude toward life.

One is tempted to comment in the words of Shakespeare —

> But as imagination bodies forth
> The forms of things unknown, the poet's pen
> Turns them to shapes and gives to airy nothing
> A local habitation and a name.

This would seem to be a very adequate description of Professor Dewey's idea of the incarnation. It remains to be seen, however, whether the thought of " airy nothing " becoming flesh and dwelling among us really marks an improvement upon the concept of the Logos.

It does not require profound knowledge of human psychology or vast experience of life to understand why the imagination can never provide a basis for a common faith. It might provide the basis for a common national faith or a common class faith but never for a universal faith. It cannot do this simply because it is man's imagination, and the social environment conditions man's imagination more than any other single factor. The human imagination, unconditioned by the Christian faith, invariably reflects the dominant social forces in which the individual is interested. If the dominant forces in any day are national forces the imagination will above all reflect the national ethos.

It will be the national ethos that will inform the imagination and enflame it. The normal thing to expect of a child brought up in present day Germany is that its imagination will be fed by the Nazi faith. By the grace of God through Christ that child as he grows to manhood may be able to rise above the social forces that surround him and at the risk of his life assert his citizenship in Christendom. But that assertion would be a flat denial of the adequacy of Professor Dewey's definition. For it would mean that the religious attitude of this particular individual had impelled him to repudiate the ideal ends which his natural German imagination had presented to him, and to act in the interest of other ends incapable of being reconciled with the ends presented by that imagination.

Professor Dewey has accepted without any qualification Rousseau's doctrine of man. He feels thoroughly satisfied with a religious attitude derived from the human imagination because he believes that all men everywhere are naturally good. Consequently, he trusts man's good imagination to present him with inclusive ideal ends. Even 1914 has not shattered Professor Dewey's sublimely naïve faith in man. His mind has been hypnotized by Rousseau's entrancing vision " that man is naturally good and that our social institutions alone have rendered him evil." This constitutes the tragedy of Professor Dewey's ventures into philosophy and religion.

Rousseau's doctrine of man is the curse of the age in which we live. It has become a curse because it has been accepted as true, whereas it is palpably untrue. The application of the scientific method to the facts of contemporary life or even the impartial eye of a realistic observer will furnish ample evidence that men are not naturally good. Yet we are witnesses to the amazing spectacle of the uncritical acceptance of this unscientific and romantic assumption by men who, in every other sphere of life, pride themselves upon their devotion to evidence presented by " the hard stuff of the world of physical and social experience."

The lesson of the hard stuff of social experience is perfectly plain. It is this: that the greatest evils which harass the modern world and which threaten it with destruction are the lineal descendants of the doctrine that man is naturally good. It is that false doctrine which has made man himself the end-all and be-all of existence, and which has filled the world with the cults of blood and race and nation. And in so far as that doctrine continues to dominate Western thought we may expect the recurring horrors of war and revolution, because it is a doctrine whose logic deprives mankind of a common frame of reference and in the end sets every man against every other man.

Professor Dewey supposes that by appealing to the imagination as the source of ideal ends he has suggested a religious attitude capable of supplying mankind with *a common faith*. His suggestion will have exactly the opposite effect. It will have this effect because an appeal to the imagination of the natural man in the actual world of 1935 means an appeal to national culture as the ultimate frame of reference. To suppose otherwise is the purest romanticism. And to appeal to national culture as the ultimate frame of reference is to lay the foundations not of a common faith but of a national faith. The imagination which was supposed to possess universal qualities capable of inspiring flesh and blood men of all lands and races to enter into a common faith turns out to be a specific American imagination. This is the very stuff out of which religions like the Nazi religion are eventually compounded. And that is the reason why the movement of thought which is associated with Professor Dewey's name is preparing the way for an American religion which will parallel the national religions of other countries.

Since Professor Dewey is not a Christian himself it may seem strange to devote so much space to his religious attitude in a discussion of trends in American Protestantism. The reasons for doing so are of course obvious. In a certain sense Professor Dewey sums up in his own philosophy the present stage of development of American culture. The system of thought which he represents has enormous influence throughout the country, even among people who have never heard the name of Dewey.

The extent of his influence within the Protestant church is perhaps as great as it is without the church. One only needs to remember the zeal with which Professor Wieman, in recent issues of The Christian Century, claimed Professor Dewey as a co-religionist. It is greatly to Professor Dewey's credit that he rejected Professor Wieman's overtures. He is not a theist, and the integrity of his mind forbade him to accept that designation.

An equally striking illustration of the influence within the Protestant churches of the movement of thought of which Professor Dewey is the foremost exponent is the book by Professor Baker, *Christian Missions and the New World Culture*, to which reference has already been made. This book has been hailed by the editor of The Christian Century as " the most important interpretation of Christian missions that has appeared since the modern missionary enterprise was launched, a little more than a hundred years ago." I am inclined to agree with Dr. Morrison's estimate, but for quite different reasons. Professor Baker accepts the findings of the theoretical sciences which indicate that " religion is a phase of cultural development, and missions one aspect of a more general process of culture interpenetration." If that means anything at all it means that culture, rather than the object of his worship, is the force which conditions the religious man. Form is made more significant than the content of faith. In other words, the missionary movement which Paul inaugurated was one aspect of a more general process of interpenetration between Jewish, Greek and Roman cultures. That this movement was in part a process of cultural interpenetration no one will deny. But to maintain that it was chiefly such a process is to distort the whole picture. In that event the Judaizing Christians, champions of Jewish culture, would

have made much better missionaries than Saul of
Tarsus who, in becoming Paul, ceased to be identified primarily with the Jewish tradition. The missionary Paul did not go about organizing *koinonia*
for the purpose of facilitating the cross-fertilization
of cultures, desirable as that would have been in
itself. On the contrary, the cross-fertilization of
cultures which resulted from his work was the by-
product of something else — of his announcement
of the establishment through Christ of a new world
order in which there was neither Jew nor Greek,
barbarian, Scythian, bond or free, but all were one
in Christ. St. Paul looked to Christ and his church
as the ground of unity. Professor Baker looks to
culture. That is the difference between historic
Christianity and our evolving American religion.

Having adopted culture as his frame of reference, Professor Baker heroically attempts to escape
from the limitations of national culture by positing
the emergence of a new world culture. This has
been shown to be an unjustifiable assumption.
"The hard stuff of social experience" indicates
that, regardless of what may happen in future centuries, culture in our time is a national phenomenon.
Consequently the practical effect of Professor
Baker's argument is to accelerate the domestication

of American Protestantism within the framework of American culture. What began as an attempt to universalize the message of the Protestant churches ends with the degradation of that message to the level of cross-fertilization between national cultures. Cross-fertilization between cultures is in itself a highly desirable process, but it has nothing to do with the central task of the Christian church. To confuse the process of cross-fertilization between national cultures with the mission of the Christian church is in effect to betray the faith of that church.

The names of Professor Dewey, Professor Wieman and Professor Baker are merely illustrative of what is perhaps the most significant trend in the contemporary thought of the American Protestant community. That trend is symptomatic of the world-wide disintegration of Protestantism. It means that the culture of this and other nations rather than the reality of Christendom is becoming the conditioning frame of reference for the Protestant church. In so far as this has occurred the Protestant churches of different nations have ceased to be reliable witnesses to the truth of the Christian religion.

In writing this I am not at all unmindful of the

heroic efforts that different groups within the American Protestant church have been making over a period of years to maintain their unity with their brethren in other parts of the world. Lausanne, Stockholm and Jerusalem and the movements associated with these names are monuments to the faith and courage of such Protestant leaders. My only comment would be that each of these movements is doomed to eventual failure in so far as the Protestant churches in different lands become subservient to the ends of their respective national cultures rather than to the ends of Christendom. In the face of diverging national cultures co-operation cannot continue if its only basis is a common program of activities. A common frame of reference for religious faith is the necessary condition of enduring co-operation.

If the American Protestant churches are not to betray their trust, if they are to continue to serve as reliable witnesses to the Christian faith, they must distinguish more clearly between their primary tasks and their secondary ones. We have too often mistaken secondary interests for primary obligations. Among secondary interests should be included all those interests related to the realization of the special ends of our American national culture. Under this category would come the promotion of particular programs, of particular reforms, and of particular moralities, the advocacy of this or that social formula or this or that political solution as ends in themselves.

The realization of particular purposes in our national life is the concern of Americans as citizens. Indeed, it should constitute the citizen's first concern. Moreover, if the citizen happens to be a Christian his faith will directly condition his choice of national purposes and the manner in which he relates himself to their realization. But for the Christian as Christian the realization of the ends of national culture is not his first concern. It is not his first concern because it belongs to the realm of the relative and temporal. It is an ingredient in a particular national situation. And the first task of the Christian church is not to juggle with the ingredients of that situation as if the problem of national life could be solved as one solves a jigsaw puzzle. The first task of the church is not to move these ingredients about in search of a solution, but to bring them into the presence of a new order of reality — the order of Christendom — where alone a solution in the Christian sense is possible. It is the business of the Church to remind its members that for them the ultimate frame of reference is not the aspirations of national culture but the obligations of Christendom.

The primary task of the American Protestant church is to recreate among its members belief in the reality of Christendom. That means preoccupation with those elements in the Christian faith that have an absolute and eternal value. It means the construction of a frame of reference which is at one and the same time universal in its outreach and immediately personal in its application.

This frame of reference includes —

A Christian teaching, embracing such doctrines as

> The doctrine of God.
> The doctrine of man.
> The divine drama of salvation.

A Christian society:

> The life of the Christian church as a catholic community of faith.
> The nature and function of this community.

A Christian ethic:

> The implications of Christian teaching and of the existence of a catholic community

of faith for personal and social life within the nation.

The implications of Christendom for the international order.

The choice before the American Protestant churches is plain. They must choose between the above frame of reference and the frame of reference supplied by American culture. If they choose the latter they will forfeit their right to speak in the name of the Christian faith. In so far as they continue to use that name they will be false witnesses who have betrayed their trust and are misleading the people. The Protestant churches will continue to merit confidence and support only if they choose the frame of reference supplied by the reality of Christendom. And paradoxical though it may seem, it will be only as they are faithful to that frame of reference that any culture worthy of the name will survive in America.

PART THREE

By H. Richard Niebuhr

TOWARD THE INDEPENDENCE OF
THE CHURCH

THE relation of the church to civilization is
necessarily a varying one since each of these
entities is continually changing and each is subject
to corruption and to conversion. The history of
the relationship is marked by periods of conflict, of
alliance, and of identification. A converted church
in a corrupt civilization withdraws to its upper
rooms, into monasteries and conventicles; it issues
forth from these in the aggressive evangelism of
apostles, monks and friars, circuit riders and missionaries; it relaxes its rigorism as it discerns signs
of repentance and faith; it enters into inevitable alliance with converted emperors and governors,
philosophers and artists, merchants and entrepre-
neurs, and begins to live at peace in the culture they
produce under the stimulus of their faith; when
faith loses its force, as generation follows generation, discipline is relaxed, repentance grows formal,
corruption enters with idolatry, and the church,
tied to the culture which it sponsored, suffers corruption with it. Only a new withdrawal followed
by a new aggression can then save the church and

restore to it the salt with which to savor society. This general pattern has been repeated three times in the past: in the ancient world, in the medieval, and in the modern. It may be repeated many times in the future. Yet the interest of any generation of Christians lies less in the pattern as a whole than in its own particular relation to the prevailing civilization. The character of that relation is defined not only by the peculiar character of the contemporary church and the contemporary culture but even more by the demand which the abiding gospel makes upon Christianity. The task of the present generation appears to lie in the liberation of the church from its bondage to a corrupt civilization. It would not need to be said that such an emancipation can be undertaken only for the sake of a new aggression and a new participation in constructive work, were there not so many loyal churchmen who shy away at every mention of withdrawal as though it meant surrender and flight rather than renewal and reorganization prior to battle. Their strategy calls for immediate attack, as though the church were unfettered, sure of its strength and of its plan of campaign.

In speaking of the church's emancipation from the world we do not imply, as the romantic perversion of Christianity implies, that civilization as such is worldly, in the apostolic meaning of that term. Nor do we identify the world with nature as spiritualist asceticism does. The essence of worldliness is neither civilization nor nature, but idolatry and lust. Idolatry is the worship of images instead of that which they image; it is the worship of man, the image of God, or of man's works, images of the image of God. It appears wherever finite and relative things or powers are regarded as ends-in-themselves, where man is treated as existing for his own sake, where civilization is valued for civilization's sake, where art is practiced for art's sake, where life is lived for life's sake or nation adored for nation's sake. It issues in a false morality, which sets up ideals that do not correspond to the nature of human life and promulgates laws that are not the laws of reality but the decrees of finite, self-aggrandizing and vanishing power. Worldliness may be defined in New Testament terms as the lust of the flesh, the lust of the eyes, and the pride of life. As idolatry is the perversion of worship so lust is the perversion of love. It is desire desiring itself, or desire stopping short of its true object, seeking satisfaction in that which is merely the symbol of the satisfactory. It is pride, the perversion of faith, since it is faith in self instead of the faith of a self in that which gives meaning to selfhood. Such worldliness is far more dangerous to man in civilization than in primitive life because of the interdependence of developed society and the power of its units. The temptation to idolatry and lust is the greater the more man is surrounded by the works of his own hands. Moreover, every civilization is conditioned in all its forms by its faith, be it idolatrous or divine, so that it is difficult to draw a precise line between culture and religion. Nevertheless, Christianity regards worldliness rather than civilization as the foe of the gospel and of men; it rejects the ascetic and romantic efforts to solve life's problems by flight from civilization.

Idolatry and lust can be directed to many things. Worldliness is protean; understood and conquered in one form it assumes another and yet another. In contemporary civilization it appears as a humanism which regards man as existing for his own sake and which makes him the object of his own worship. It appears also as a nationalism in which man is taught to live and die for his own race or country as the ultimate worthful reality, and which requires the promotion of national power and glory at the expense of other nations as well as of the individuals with their own direct relation to the eternal. It has exhibited itself in the guise of a capitalism for which wealth is the great creative and redemptive power, and as an industrialism which worships the tawdry products of human hands as the sources of life's meaning. Humanity, nation, wealth, industry — these are all but finite entities, neither good nor bad in themselves; in their rightful place they become ministers to the best; regarded and treated as self-sufficient and self-justifying they become destructive to self and others. In the modern world they have become ends-in-themselves. A culture which was made possible only by the liberation of men from ancient idolatries and lusts has succumbed to its own success. It is not merely a secular culture, as though it had simply eliminated religion from its government, business, art and education. It has not eliminated faith but substituted a worldly for a divine faith. It has a religion which, like most religion, is bad — an idolatrous faith which brings with it a train of moral consequences, destructive of the lives of its devotees and damning them to a hell of dissatisfaction, inner conflict, war and barbarism as lurid as any nether region which the imagination of the past conceived.

The church allied with the civilization in which this idolatry prevails has become entangled not only in its culture but also in its worldliness. This captivity of the church is the first fact with which we need to deal in our time.

I

The Captive Church

The church is in bondage to capitalism. Capitalism in its contemporary form is more than a system of ownership and distribution of economic goods. It is a faith and a way of life. It is faith in wealth as the source of all life's blessings and as the savior of man from his deepest misery. It is the doctrine that man's most important activity is the production of economic goods and that all other things are dependent upon this. On the basis of this initial idolatry it develops a morality in which economic worth becomes the standard by which to measure all other values and the economic virtues take precedence over courage, temperance, wisdom and justice, over charity, humility and fidelity. Hence nature, love, life, truth, beauty and justice are exploited or made the servants of the high economic good. Everything, including the lives of workers, is made a utility, is desecrated and ultimately destroyed. Capitalism develops a discipline of its own but in the long run makes for the overthrow of all discipline since the service of its god demands the encouragement of unlimited desire for that which promises — but must fail — to satisfy the lust of the flesh and the pride of life.

The capitalist faith is not a disembodied spirit. It expresses itself in laws and social habits and transforms the whole of civilization. It fashions society into an economic organization in which production for profit becomes the central enterprise, in which the economic relations of men are regarded as their fundamental relations, in which economic privileges are most highly prized, and in which the resultant classes of men are set to struggle with one another for the economic goods. Education and government are brought under the sway of the faith. The family itself is modified by it. The structure of cities and their very architecture is influenced by the religion. So intimate is the relation between the civilization and the faith, that it is difficult to participate in the former without consenting to the latter and becoming entangled in its destructive morality. It was possible for

Paul's converts to eat meat which had been offered to idols without compromising with paganism. But the products which come from the altars of this modern idolatry — the dividends, the privileges, the status, the struggle — are of such a sort that it is difficult to partake of them without becoming involved in the whole system of misplaced faith and perverted morality.[1]

No antithesis could be greater than that which obtains between the gospel and capitalist faith. The church has known from the beginning that the love of money is the root of evil, that it is impossible to serve God and Mammon, that they that have riches shall hardly enter into life, that life does not consist in the abundance of things possessed, that the earth is the Lord's and that love, not self-interest,

[1] The theory that modern capitalism is a system with a religious foundation and a cultural superstructure obviously runs counter to the widely accepted Marxian doctrine. It is not our intention to deny many elements in the Marxian analysis: the reality of the class struggle, the destructive self-contradiction in modern capitalism, the effect of capitalism upon government, law, the established religion. Neither are we intent upon defending the principle of private property as an adequate basis for the modern economic structure. But we are implying that modern capitalism does not represent the inevitable product of the private property system in which early democracy and Puritanism were interested, that it has corrupted and perverted that system, making of it something which it was never intended to be nor was bound to be. We believe that the economic interpretation of history is itself a product and a statement of the economic faith and that communism is in many ways a variant form of capitalist religion.

is the first law of life. Yet the church has become
entangled with capitalist civilization to such an extent that it has compromised with capitalist faith
and morality and become a servant of the world.
So intimate have the bonds between capitalism and
Protestantism become that the genealogists have
suspected kinship. Some have ascribed the par-
entage of capitalism to Protestantism while others
have seen in the latter the child of the former. But
whatever may have been the relation between the
modest system of private ownership which a Calvin
or a Wesley allowed and the gospel they proclaimed, that which obtains between the high capitalism of the later period and the church must fall
under the rule of the seventh and not of the fifth
commandment, as a Hosea or a Jeremiah would
have been quick to point out. The entanglement
with capitalism appears in the great economic interests of the church, in its debt structure, in its
dependence through endowments upon the continued dividends of capitalism, and especially in
its dependence upon the continued gifts of the
privileged classes in the economic society. This
entanglement has become the greater the more the
church has attempted to keep pace with the development of capitalistic civilization, not without

compromising with capitalist ideas of success and efficiency. At the same time evidence of religious syncretism, of the combination of Christianity with capitalist religion, has appeared. The "building of the kingdom of God" has been confused in many a churchly pronouncement with the increase of church possessions or with the economic advancement of mankind. The church has often behaved as though the saving of civilization and particularly of capitalist civilization were its mission. It has failed to apply to the morality of that civilization the rigid standards which it did not fail to use where less powerful realities were concerned. The development may have been inevitable, nevertheless it was a fall.

The bondage of the church to nationalism has been more apparent than its bondage to capitalism, partly because nationalism is so evidently a religion, partly because it issues in the dramatic sacrifices of war — sacrifices more obvious if not more actual than those which capitalism demands and offers to its god. Nationalism is no more to be confused with the principle of nationality than capitalism is to be confused with the principle of private property. Just as we can accept, without complaint against the past, the fact that a private

132

property system replaced feudalism, so we can accept, without blaming our ancestors for moral delinquency, the rise of national organization in place of universal empire. But as the private property system became the soil in which the lust for possessions and the worship of wealth grew up, so the possibility of national independence provided opportunity for the growth of religious nationalism, the worship of the nation, and the lust for national power and glory. And as religious capitalism perverted the private property system, so religious nationalism corrupted the nationalities. Nationalism regards the nation as the supreme value, the source of all life's meaning, as an end-in-itself and a law to itself. It seeks to persuade individuals and organizations to make national might and glory their main aim in life. It even achieves a certain deliverance of men by freeing them from their bondage to self. In our modern polytheism it enters into close relationship with capitalism, though not without friction and occasional conflict, and sometimes it appears to offer an alternative faith to those who have become disillusioned with wealth-worship. Since the adequacy of its god is continually called into question by the existence of other national deities, it requires the demonstration of the omnipotence of nation and breeds an unlimited lust for national power and expansion. But since the god is limited the result is conflict, war and destruction. Despite the fact that the nationalist faith becomes obviously dominant only in times of sudden or continued political crisis, it has had constant and growing influence in the West, affecting particularly government and education.

The antithesis between the faith of the church and the nationalist idolatry has always been self-evident. The prophetic revolution out of which Christianity eventually came was a revolution against nationalist religion. The messianic career of Jesus developed in defiance of the nationalisms of Judaism and of Rome. In one sense Christianity emerged out of man's disillusionment with the doctrine that the road to life and joy and justice lies through the exercise of political force and the growth of national power. The story of its rise is the history of long struggle with self-righteous political power. Yet in the modern world Christianity has fallen into dependence upon the political agencies which have become the instruments of nationalism and has compromised with the religion they promote. The division of Christendom into national units would have been a less serious matter had it not resulted so frequently in a division into nationalistic units. The close relation of church and state in some instances, the participation of the church in the political life in other cases, has been accompanied by a syncretism of nationalism and Christianity. The confusion of democracy with the Christian ideal of life in America, of racialism and the gospel in Germany, of Western nationalism and church missions in the Orient, testify to the compromise which has taken place. The churches have encouraged the nations to regard themselves as messianic powers and have supplied them with religious excuses for their imperialist expansions and aggressions. And in every time of crisis it has been possible for nationalism to convert the major part of the church, which substituted the pagan Baal for the great Jehovah, without being well aware of what it did, and promoted a holy crusade in negation of the cross. The captivity of the church to the world of nationalism does not assume so dramatic a form as a rule, yet the difficulty of Christianity in achieving an international organization testifies to the reality of its bondage.

Capitalism and nationalism are variant forms of a faith which is more widespread in modern civilization than either. It is difficult to label this religion. It may be called humanism, but there is a humanism that, far from glorifying man, reminds him of his limitations the while it loves him in his feebleness and aspiration. It has become fashionable to name it liberalism, but there is a liberalism which is interested in human freedom as something to be achieved rather than something to be assumed and praised. It may be called modernism, but surely one can live in the modern world, accepting its science and engaging in its work, without falling into idolatry of the modern. The rather too technical term "anthropocentrism" seems to be the best designation of the faith. It is marked on its negative side by the rejection not only of the symbols of the creation, the fall and the salvation of men, but also of the belief in human dependence and limitation, in human wickedness and frailty, in divine forgiveness through the suffering of the innocent. Positively it affirms the sufficiency of man. Human desire is the source of all values. The mind and the will of man are sufficient instruments of his salvation. Evil is nothing but lack of development. Revolutionary second-birth is unnecessary. Although some elements of the anthropocentric faith are always present in human society, and although it was represented at the beginning of the modern development, it is not the source but rather the product of modern civilization. Growing out of the success of science and technology in understanding and modifying some of the conditions of life, it has substituted veneration of science for scientific knowledge, and glorification of human activity for its exercise. Following upon the long education in which Protestant and Catholic evangelism had brought Western men to a deep sense of their duty, this anthropocentrism glorified the moral sense of man as his natural possession and taught him that he needed no other law than the one within. Yet, as in the case of capitalism and nationalism, the faith which grew out of modern culture has modified that culture. During the last generations the anthropocentric faith has entered deeply into the structure of society and has contributed not a little to the megapolitanism and megalomania of contemporary civilization.

The compromise of the church with anthropocentrism has come almost imperceptibly in the course of its collaboration in the work of culture. It was hastened by the tenacity of Christian traditionalism, which appeared to leave churchmen with no alternative than one between worship of the letter and worship of the men who wrote the letters. Nevertheless, the compromise is a perversion of the Christian position. The more obvious expressions of the compromise have been frequent but perhaps less dangerous than the prevailing one by means of which Christianity appeared to remain true to itself while accepting the anthropocentric position. That compromise was the substitution of religion for the God of faith. Man's aspiration after God, his prayer, his worship was exalted in this syncretism into a saving power, worthy of a place alongside science and art. Religion was endowed with all the attributes of Godhead, the while its basis was found in human nature itself. The adaptation of Christianity to the anthropocentric faith appeared in other ways: in the attenuation of the conviction of sin and of the necessity of rebirth, in the substitution of the human claim to immortality for the Christian hope and fear of an after-life, in the glorification of religious heroes, and in the efforts of religious men and societies to become saviors.

The captive church is the church which has become entangled with this system or these systems of worldliness. It is a church which seeks to prove its usefulness to civilization, in terms of civilization's own demands. It is a church which has lost the distinctive note and the earnestness of a Christian discipline of life and has become what every religious institution tends to become — the teacher of the prevailing code of morals and the pantheon of the social gods. It is a church, moreover, which has become entangled with the world in its desire for the increase of its power and prestige and which shares the worldly fear of insecurity.

How the church became entangled and a captive in this way may be understood. To blame the past for errors which have brought us to this pass is to indulge in the ancient fallacy of saying that the fathers have eaten sour grapes and the children's teeth are set on edge. The function of the present is neither praise nor blame of the past. It is rather the realization of the prevailing situation and preparation for the next task.

II

The Revolt in the Church

The realization of the dependence of the church is widespread and has led to revolt. There is revolt against the church and revolt within the church. Both of these uprisings have various aspects. The revolt against the church is in part the rebellion of those who have found in Christianity only the pure traditionalism of doctrine and symbol which have become meaningless through constant repetition without rethinking and through the consequent substitution of symbol for reality. In part it is a revulsion against the sentimentality which substituted for the ancient symbols, with the realities to which they pointed, the dubious realities of man's inner religious and moral life. In part it is the revolt of those who see in the church the willing servitor of tyrannical social institutions and classes. On the one hand, the intellectuals abandon the church because of its traditionalism or romanticism; on the other hand, disinherited classes and races protest against it as the ally of capitalist, racial or nationalist imperialism. But these revolts against the church are not the most significant elements in the present situation, from the church's point of view. They represent desertions and attacks inspired not by loyalty to the church's own principles but rather by devotion to interests other than those of the church. Such desertions and attacks, however justified they may seem from certain points of view, serve only to weaken the church and to increase its dependence. Only a churchly revolt can lead to the church's independence.

The revolt within the church has a dual character. It is a revolt both against the " world " of contemporary civilization and against the secularized church. No other institution or society in the Western world seems to be so shot through with the spirit of rebellion against the secular system with its abuses, as is the church. No other institution seems to harbor within it so many rebels against its own present form. They are rebels who are fundamentally loyal — loyal, that is to say, to the essential institution while they protest against its corrupted form. They have no alternative religions or philosophies of life to which they might wish to flee. A few, to be sure, leave the church year by year, yet even among these loyalty is often manifest. Some of the rebels remain romanticists who try to build " a kingdom of God " with secular means. More of them are frustrated revolutionaries who hate " the world " which outrages their consciences and denies their faith but who know of no way in which they can make their rebellion effective or by which they can reconcile themselves to the situation.

141

Like every revolt in its early stages, the Christian revolution of today is uncertain of its ends and vague in its strategy. It seems to be a sentiment and a protest rather than a theory and a plan of action. It is a matter of feeling, in part, just because the situation remains unanalyzed. It issues therefore in many ill-tempered accusations and in blind enthusiasms. Sometimes it concentrates itself against some particular feature of the secular civilization which seems particularly representative of its character. Perhaps the crusade against the liquor traffic was indebted for some of its force to the uneasy conscience of a church which was able to treat this particular phase of the " world " as the symbol and representative of all worldliness. As in all such emotional revolts there is a temptation to identify the evil with some evildoer and to make individual men — capitalists, munitions-manufacturers, dictators — responsible for the situation. Thus early Christians may have dealt with Nero, and Puritans with popes. The confusion of the revolt in the church is apparent, however, not only in its emotionalism but also in its association with revolting groups outside the church. In the beginning of every uprising against prevailing customs and institutions disparate groups who share a common antagonism are likely to assume that they share a common loyalty. It was so when princes and protestants and peasants arose against the Roman church and empire; it was so also when Puritans, Presbyterians, Independents and sectarians rose against King Charles. Dissenters and democrats united in opposing the established church in American colonies. Such groups are united in their negations, not in their affirmations. Their positive loyalties, for the sake of which they make a common rejection, may be wholly different. The revolt in the church against the " world " and against " the world in the church " is confused to-day because of such associations. This confusion implies perils and temptations which may lead to disaster or to the continued captivity of the church. For if it is a frequent experience that common antagonism is confused with common loyalty, it is also well known that allies are prone to fight among themselves because of their variant interests. One danger to the Christian revolt is that it will enter into alliance with forces whose aims and strategies are so foreign to its own that when the common victory is won — if won it can be — the revolutionary church will be left with the sad reflection that it supplied the " Fourteen Points " which gave specious sanctity to an outrageous peace and that its fruits of victory are an external prosperity based on rotting foundations and debts which it cannot collect without destroying its own life

The danger of such alliance or identification is not a fancied peril. The eagerness with which some of the leaders of the Christian revolt identify the gospel with the ideals and strategies of radical political parties, whether they be proletarian or nationalistic, the efforts to amalgamate gospel and political movements in a Christian socialism or in a Christian nationalism indicate the reality of the danger. It is not always understood by the American section of the Christian revolt that a considerable section of the so-called German Christian movement, in which the confusion of gospel and nationalism prevails, had sources in just such a reaction as its own against an individualistic, profit-loving and capitalistic civilization, and against the church in alliance with that civilization. There are many social idealists among these Germanizers of the gospel; and their fervor is essentially like that of the other idealists who equate the kingdom of God with a proletarian socialist instead of a national socialist society. The " social gospel," in so far as it is the identification of the gospel with a certain temporal order, is no recent American invention. In the history of Europe and America there have been many similar efforts which sought ideal ends, identified the church with political agencies, and succeeded in fastening upon society only some new form of power control against which the church needed again to protest and rebel. Christianity has been confused in the past, in situations more or less similar to the present, with the rule of the Roman Empire, with feudalism, with the divine right of kings, with the rule of majorities, with the dominance of the Northern States over the Southern, with the extension of Anglo-Saxon influence in the Orient. The confusion was as explicable and as specious in every instance as is the identification of Christianity with radical political movements today. Yet in every instance the result was a new tyranny, a new disaster and a new dependence of the church. It is one thing for Christians to take a responsible part in the political life of their nation; it is another thing to identify the gospel and its antagonism to the " world " with the " worldly " antagonism of some revolting group.

The common social ideal or hope of the West includes the establishment of liberty, equality, fraternity, justice and peace. Almost every revolting movement in the past as well as in the present has fought in the name of this ideal and sought to establish it. With the ideal, Christianity cannot but have profound sympathy, for Christianity taught it first of all to the Western world. But every political and social revolt is based on the belief that the ideal can be established through the exercise of power by a disinterested group or person, be it the feudal group, the monarch, the middle class or the proletariat. To identify Christianity with one form of the messianic delusion and of the philosophy of power, while rejecting another, is to be guilty of emotional and wishful thinking. In so far as every new revolt is an attack upon the philosophy and structure of power politics and self-righteousness, Christianity cannot but sympathize with it; in so far as it is itself a new form of the philosophy, Christianity must reject it or at least refuse to identify itself with it. So long, of course, as the church has no faith in a divine revolution and no strategy of its own for participation in that revolution it will need to commit itself to some other revolutionary faith and strategy or remain conservative. But in such a case it can have no true existence as a church; it can function only as the religious institution of a revolting society, serving the interests of the society in the same way that a capitalist church serves a capitalist society.

The revolt in the church faces another danger in consequence of the tendency toward the identification of Christianity with revolting secular movements. Multitudes of Christians who had become aware of tension between the gospel and the world but who are also aware of the irreconcilability of the Christian faith with the faiths of communism, socialism or fascism are forced to make a choice between impossible alternatives. The greater part of them are driven into reaction, for the old identification of Christianity with the prevailing " worldliness " is at least more familiar to them than the new. The fruit of false action today in Christianity as in civilization will be reaction, not a true revolution. Similar movements in the past offer unmistakable lessons on this point. The confusion of Christian and of political Puritanism played no small part in bringing on the Restoration. The identification of the protest against slavery with the interests of the Northern States drove many Christians in the South to the defense of the " peculiar institution," made the Civil

War inevitable and contributed to the continuation of the race problem. There is no guarantee that reaction can be avoided under any circumstances, but it may be held in check. There is no guarantee that overt struggle can be avoided, but it is criminal to make civil, class or international war the more likely by confusing issues and by arousing the passions which religious fervor can awaken. And in the end the solution will be as little to the mind of Christians as the unsolved problem was.

The dangers and temptations which beset the Christian revolt offer no excuse for acquiescence. The danger which confronts the world in the midst of its idolatries and lusts is too real, the message of the church is too imperative, the misery of men is too actual to make quiescence possible. But the moment requires the church to stand upon its own feet, to do its work in its own way, to carry on its revolt against " the world," not in dependence upon allies or associates, but independently. In any case the revolt in the church against secularization of life and the system of " worldliness " points the way to the declaration of its independence.

III

TOWARD THE INDEPENDENCE OF THE CHURCH

The declaration of the church's independence, when it comes, will not begin on the negative note. A movement toward emancipation cannot become effective so long as it is only a rejection of false loyalties and entanglements. Loyalties can be recognized to be false only when a true loyalty has been discovered. Moreover, independence is not desirable for its own sake. To seek it for its own sake means to seek it for the sake of self and to substitute loyalty to a self-sufficient self for loyalty to an alien power. But the church can have no illusion of self-sufficiency. Neither can it trust itself to play a messianic role in the deliverance of mankind. It knows too well that hierocracies have not been shining examples of justice among the aristocracies, monarchies, democracies, plutocracies, race tyrannies and class rules which have oppressed mankind.

The church's declaration of independence can begin only with the self-evident truth that it and all life are dependent upon God, that loyalty to him is the condition of life and that to him belong

149

the kingdom and the power and the glory. Otherwise the emancipation of the church from the world
is impossible; there is no motive for it nor any
meaning in it. There is no flight out of the captivity of the church save into the captivity of God.
Such words must seem to many to be pious and
meaningless platitudes, mere gestures of respect to
the past and bare of that realism which the present
moment demands. That this is so is but another
illustration of the extent to which the faith of the
church has been confounded with the belief in the
ideas, wishes and sentiments of men, and to which
the word *God* has been made the symbol, not of
the last reality with which man contends, but of
his own aspirations. It remains true that loyalty
to the " I am that I am " is the only reason for the
church's existence and that the recovery of this
loyalty is the beginning of true emancipation. It
is even more true that this loyalty is not our own
creation but that through the destruction of our
idols and the relentless pursuit of our self-con-
fidence God is driving us, in the church and in the
world, to the last stand where we must recognize
our dependence upon him or, in vainglorious rebellion, suffer demoralization and dissolution. The
crisis of modern mankind is like the crisis of

the prophets, the crisis of the Roman Empire in the days of Augustine, and that of the medieval world in the days of the Reformation. The last appeal beyond all finite principalities and powers must soon be made. It cannot be an appeal to the rights of men, of nations or religions but only an appeal to the right of God.

The appeal to the right of God means for the church an appeal to the right of Jesus Christ. It is an appeal not only to the grim reality of the slayer who judges and destroys the self-aggrandizing classes and nations and men. Such an appeal would be impossible and such a loyalty out of question were not men persuaded that this reality, whose ways are again evident in historic processes, is a redeeming and saving reality, and did they not come to some understanding of the manner in which he accomplishes salvation. But such persuasion and such revelation are available only through the event called Jesus Christ. If the church has no other plan of salvation to offer to men than one of deliverance by force, education, idealism or planned economy, it really has no existence as a church and needs to resolve itself into a political party or a school. But it knows of a plan of salvation which is not a plan it has devised. In its revolt it is becoming aware of the truth which it had forgotten or which it had hidden within symbols and myths. There is in the revolt something of the restlessness that comes from a buried memory which presses into consciousness. In some of its aspects it seems to be the blind effort to escape from the knowledge that the church along with the world belongs to the crucifiers rather than to the crucified. It seems to represent the desire to avert the eyes from the cross which stands in the present as in the past, and to turn attention away from ourselves to some other culprits whose sins the innocent must bear. When this memory of Jesus Christ, the crucified, comes fully alive it will not come as a traditional formula or symbol, reminding men only of the past, but as the recollection of a most decisive fact in the present situation of men. The church's remembrance of Jesus Christ will come in contemporary terms, so that it will be able to say: "That which was from the beginning, that which we have heard, that which we have seen with our eyes, that which we have beheld and which our hands have handled concerning the Word of life — that declare we unto you."

Without this beginning in loyalty to God and

to Jesus Christ no new beginning of the church's life is possible. But the self-evident truths and the original loyalties of the church can be recaptured and reaffirmed not only as the events in time drive men to their reaffirmation, but as the labor of thought makes intelligible and clear the vague and general perceptions we receive from life. The dependent church rejected theology or found it unintelligible because it accepted a " theology " which was not its own, a theory of life which was essentially worldly. It wanted action rather than creeds because its creed was that the action of free, intelligent men was good and that God's action was limited to human agencies of good will. The revolters in the church are learning that without a Christian theory or theology the Christian movement must lose itself in emotions and sentiments or hasten to action which will be premature and futile because it is not based upon a clear analysis of the situation. They have learned from the communists that years spent in libraries and in study are not necessarily wasted years but that years of activity without knowledge are lost years indeed. They have learned from history that every true work of liberation and reformation was at the same time a work of theology. They understand that the dependence of man upon God and the orientation of man's work by reference to God's work require that theology must take the place of the psychology and sociology which were the proper sciences of a Christianity which was dependent on the spirit in man. The theory of the Christian revolution is beginning to unfold itself again as the theory of a divine determinism, of the inevitable divine judgment, and of the salvation of men by the suffering of the innocent. But whatever be the content of the theory a clear understanding of it is needed for the work of emancipation, reorganization and aggression in the Christian community.

It is evident that far more than all this is necessary. There is no easy way in which the church can divorce itself from the world. It cannot flee into asceticism nor seek refuge again in the inner life of the spirit. The road to independence and to aggression is not one which leads straight forward upon one level. How to be in the world and yet not of the world has always been the problem of the church. It is a revolutionary community in a pre-revolutionary society. Its main task always remains that of understanding, proclaiming and preparing for the divine revolution in human life. Nevertheless, there remains the necessity of participation in the affairs of an unconverted and unreborn world. Hence the church's strategy always has a dual character and the dualism is in constant danger of being resolved into the monism of other-worldliness or of this-worldliness, into a more or less quiescent expectancy of a revolution beyond time or of a mere reform program carried on in terms of the existent order. How to maintain the dualism without sacrifice of the main revolutionary interest constitutes one of the important problems of a church moving toward its independence.

Yet it is as futile as it is impossible to project at this moment the solution of problems which will arise in the future. If the future is pregnant with difficulties it is no less full of promise. The movement toward the independence of the church may lead to the development of a new missionary or evangelical movement, to the rise of an effective international Christianity, to the union of the divided parts of the church of Christ, and to the realization in civilization of the unity and peace of the saved children of one God. The fulfilment of hopes and fears cannot be anticipated. The future will vary according to the way in which we deal with the present. And in this present the next step only begins to be visible. The time seems rife for the declaration of the church's independence. Yet even that step cannot be forced; how it will come and under what leadership none can now determine. We can be sure, however, that the repentance and faith working in the rank and file of the church are the preconditions of its independence and renewal.